NI Key Stage 3
English Year 9

Series Editor: **Kate O'Hanlon**

Authors: **Noreen Doran**, **Vanessa Goucher**, **Maura Johnston** and **Jennifer Magowan**

HODDER
EDUCATION
PART OF HACHETTE LIVRE UK

Although every effort has been made to ensure that website addresses are correct at time of going to press, Hodder Education cannot be held responsible for the content of any website mentioned in this book. It is sometimes possible to find a relocated web page by typing in the address of the home page for a website in the URL window of your browser.

Hachette's policy is to use papers that are natural, renewable and recyclable products and made from wood grown in sustainable forests. The logging and manufacturing processes are expected to conform to the environmental regulations of the country of origin.

Orders: please contact Bookpoint Ltd, 130 Milton Park, Abingdon, Oxon OX14 4SB. Telephone: (44) 01235 827720. Fax: (44) 01235 400454. Lines are open 9.00 – 5.00, Monday to Saturday, with a 24-hour message answering service. Visit our website at www.hoddereducation.co.uk

Cover photo © Mitchell Funk / Photographer's Choice / Getty Images
Illustrations by Jane Gerwitz and Bob Moulder
Typeset in Helvetica Neue Light in 11pt by Starfish Design Editorial and Project Management Ltd
Printed and bound in Italy

A catalogue record for this title is available from the British Library

ISBN: 978 0340 876 886

Contents

Unit 1: Magical landscapes

Unit 2: No stranger here

Unit 3: Reading film

Unit 4: Just a minute, let me explain...

Contents

Introduction

Welcome to your English textbook for Year 9. We hope that you will enjoy the range of texts and activities in the different units. However, we expect that you will be adding to your reading and writing experiences by using other materials for English and by reading widely from fiction and non-fiction texts. We hope that what you are learning in English will be used by you in other areas of the curriculum, and in situations beyond school.

Each of the units will address *knowledge*, *understanding* and which will extend your ability to use language effectively, communicate your ideas powerfully and understand the ideas and meanings of others.

The textbook has been written to support the learning intentions outlined within the English Learning Area of the Revised Northern Ireland Curriculum for Key Stage 3. The eight units will provide samples of fiction, non-fiction texts, poetry and drama experiences and will look at the meaning and language of moving image texts. You will be encouraged to use a wide range of modern technology in order to communicate, construct text and research new information.

While understanding of the language conventions and rules will be integrated within the work, it will be important that the structures of language be discussed explicitly and the skills applied in practical, real-life situations.

Thinking will be linked to language and opportunities will be available for you to:

- manage information
- think, problem-solve and take decisions
- be creative
- manage yourself
- work with others.

Learning Intentions for English

Learning Intentions	Words used to describe Learning Intentions in English strand
Managing information	Research and manage information effectively, using Mathematics and ICT where appropriate
Thinking, problem solving, decision making	Show deeper understanding by thinking critically and flexibly, solving problems and making informed decisions, using Mathematics and ICT where appropriate
Being creative	Demonstrate creativity and initiative when developing ideas and following them through
Working with others	Work effectively with others
Self management	Demonstrate self management by working systematically, persisting with tasks, evaluating and improving own performance

Features of the book

Beginning work

Each unit will show two boxes at the top of the page:
- What we will be doing
- What we will be learning.

These will make clear the purposes of each unit.

Writing

It will help if you are clear about the following:

Purpose: Why am I writing? What genre of writing will be suitable for my purpose – recount, instruction, explanation, narrative?

Audience: To whom or for whom am I writing? What form of writing will be most suitable – letter, diary, story, email, video, news article, magazine?

Word definitions

In many places you will find dictionary definitions of the words used in that part of the book. This will help you get on quickly and successfully with the work you are doing.

Talking and listening

Many activities will ask you to work in pairs or small groups. This will help you to learn and think more successfully.

ICT

We hope you will pick up and develop suggestions made about the use of:
- computers
- software
- the internet
- film
- video/DVD
- audio texts
- radio.

Reading

Texts in a wide range of genres and forms will be provided. Let them motivate you to read more. You may be guided by suggestions made for extended reading.

Self-assessment

At the end of each unit you will be asked:
- What have you learned?
- What are your next goals for improvement?

This will help develop your skills.

Developing your thinking

You will be given many opportunities to think about your own thinking processes and skills. The work will ask you to be a creative and critical thinker. Problem solving will be an element of each unit of work.

The Publishers would like to thank the following for permission to reproduce copyright material:

Photo credits (*t* = top, *b* = bottom, *l* = left, *r* = right) **p.2** *l* ©Simon Brown/Alamy, *r* ©Paul Wakefield/The National Trust Photo Library/Alamy, *b* ©Craig Hiller/Alamy; **p.3** ©Waldron Media/Disney/The Ronald Grant Archive; **p.6** ©Courtesy Waldron Media/Disney/Ronald Grant Archive; **p.7** ©Eoin Colfer, Used with kind permission on Penguin UK; **p.8** ©Richard Cummins/Corbis; **p.13** ©Huw John/Rex Features; **p.14** *t* ©, Phoenix Photography, *b* ©Disney/The Ronald Grant Archive; **p.15** *t-b* ©Colin McPherson/Corbis, ©Hans Wild/Time Life Pictures/Getty Images, ©Richard Gardner/Rex Features; **p.19** ©Denis Felix/Corbis; **p.23 & 24** ©Maura Johnston, used with kind permission; **p.30** main ©Richard Young/Rex Features, inset ©Andrew Holt/Alamy; **p.31** ©W. Disney/Everett/Rex Features; **p.36** ©Columbia/Everett/Rex Features; **p.41** ©Nicola Campbell/Alamy; **p.42** ©Angello Picco/Rex Features; **p.43** ©Warner Bros/Everett/Rex Features; **p.44** ©Warner Bros & J K Rowling/The Ronald Grant Archive; **p.53** ©Phoenix Photography; **p.54** *l* ©Joe Ravetz, Centre for Urban & Regional Ecology, School of Environment & Development, HBS, Manchester University, used with kind permission, *r* Reproduced from Northern Limits - a resource flow analysis and ecological footprint for Northern Ireland, with kind permission of ARENA Network - the environmental arm of Business in the Community Northern Ireland.; **p.60** *l* ©Willi Schneider/Rex Features, *r* ©Peter Brooker/Rex Features; **p.61** ©Everett Collection/Rex Features; **p.65** ©20th Century Fox/Everett/Rex Features; **p.66** ©Photos 12/Alamy; **p.71** ©The Ronald Grant Archive; **p.73** ©Justin Kase/Alamy; **p.78** ©KPA Honorar & Belege/Content Mine International/Alamy; **p.86** ©Marwood Jenkins/Alamy; **p.91** *l* ©John Springer Collection/Corbis, *r* ©Hulton-Deutsch Collection/Corbis; **p.94** ©Bettmann/Corbis; **p.103** *l* ©JP Laffont/Sygma/Corbis, *r* ©Alan Lewis/Photopress Belfast/Corbis Sygma; **p.105** *l* ©Interfoto Pressebildagentur/Alamy, *r* ©Tim Graham/Alamy; **p.106** ©Reuters/Corbis; **p.108** ©Rainer Unkel/vario images GmbH & Co.KG/Alamy; **p.111** *l* ©Sipa Press/Rex Features, *r* ©Graham Tim/Corbis Sygma; **p.114** ©Camilla Morandi/Rex Features; **p.116** *l* ©Everett Collection/Rex Features, *r* ©KPA Honorar & Belege/Content Mine International/Alamy; **p.130** ©Kevin Johnson, used with kind permission

Acknowledgements (*t* = top, *b* = bottom, *c* = centre, *l* = left, *r* = right) **p.3 & pp4-5** The Lion, The Witch and the Wardrobe by C.S. Lewis copyright ©C.S. Lewis Pte. Ltd. 1950; **p.8 & pp9-11** extract from Artemis Fowl ©Eoin Colfer, Used with kind permission on Penguin UK; **p.20** *t-b* 'Speedwell' ©Leon McAuley, used with kind permission, 'Phemios & Medon' ©Michael Longley, used with permission of Random House, ©Seamus Heaney, The Other Side from Wintering Out, Faber and Faber Ltd, Giving Shine' from Ness Wood Nature Notes ©Ann McKay, used with kind permission Summer Palace Press; **p.22** 'Shancoduff' by Patrick Kavanagh is reprinted from Collected Poems, edited by Antoinette Quinn (Allen Lane, 2004), by kind permission of the Trustees of the Estate of the late Katherine B. Kavanagh, through the Jonathan Williams Literary Agency; **p.23** ©Louis MacNeice, 'Carrickfergus', Collected Poems, Faber, used with kind permission of David Higham Associates; **p.24** 'Mowillian' ©Maura Johnston, Lohnra Press; **pp.25-27** 'The Lad' ©W F Marshall, used with the kind permission of The Marshall Family, Castlerock, Northern Ireland; **p.33** online review of 'At World's End ©Mirrorpix, used with kind permission; **p.49** 'What is Global Warming?' ©Kay Clarke et al, Geography for CCEA GCSE (Hodder & Stoughton, 2004) Reproduced by permission of Hodder & Stoughton; **pp.50-51** 'The Water Cycle' From Badger Literacy Starters Y7 Sentence Level, by Pie Corbett, Badger Publishing Ltd.; **p.55** Adapted from Lines from the Environmental Education Forum, September 2004, used with the kind permission of Environmental Education Forum, Northern Ireland; **pp.87-88** Interview with Michael Bradley, used with kind permission of Verbal Arts Centre; **pp.90-91** 'Under Milkwood' ©Dylan Thomas, Dent, used with permission of David Higham Associates; **pp.92-93** 'Quite Early One Morning' ©Dylan Thomas, Dent, used with permission of David Higham Associates; **pp.96-97** *t* 'Blood Brothers' ©Willy Russell, A & C Black, *b* 'Observe The Sons of Ulster' ©Frank McGuinness, Faber and Faber; **pp.98-100** 'Johnny Doyle', The Sam Henry Collection is held by Belfast Central Library and used with kind permission; **p.106** George W Bush speech ©American Rhetoric.com, used with kind permission; **p.108** Tony Blair speech, used with kind permission; **p.109** Roosevelt's speech ©American Rhetoric.com, used with kind permission; **p.110** *t-b* Princess Diana's speech ©Peter Settelen, extract from speech on Eating Disorders delivered by Diana, Princess of Wales, used with the kind permission of Peter Settelen, Reagan's speech ©American Rhetoric.com, used with kind permission, Bono's speech, c/o DATA (Debt – AIDs – Trade – Africa) 111 Wardour Street, London, used with kind permission; **p.111** *t* Hillary Clinton's speech,remarks to United Nations 4th world conference on women, 5 September 1995; **p.116** *b* extract from Braveheart, Randall Wallace c/o William Morris Agency, USA; **pp.123-124** 'Royal Servant' Retold by Luis Fernandez, Copyright 2008, Amrita Bharati, Bharatiya Vidya Bhavan, Mumbai, used with kind permission; **p.127** *t* **& p.129** *b* extracts from Secret Heart ©David Almond, used with kind permission of Hodder Children's; **p.127** *b* **& 128** *b* extracts from 'Call of the Wild', Jack London; **p.128** *c* **& 129** *t* ©Helen Mc Shane, "Waiting for Daddy", My Story, ed. Pauline Currie (Blackstaff Press, 2006) reproduced by permission of the author; **p.128** *t* **& 129** *c* Licensed by David Bolt Associates, extracts from The Lost Island by Eilis Dillon; **pp.130-131** 'The Sea' ©Kevin Johnston, used with kind permission **p.132** 'Make Haste Slowly' Retold by Luis Fernandez, Copyright 2008, Amrita Bharati, Bharatiya Vidya Bhavan, Mumbai, used with kind permission.

Unit 1: Magical landscapes

What we will be doing

In this unit we will:

- work individually, in pairs and in groups
- read and discuss fiction
- prepare to read aloud for effect
- write a choice of pieces – review or creative
- read for research on local writers.

What we will be learning

In this unit we will learn to:

- understand the features of fantasy fiction
- use language with precision and for effect
- respond in writing to imaginative stimuli
- plan and write a review
- compare and contrast fiction.

Thinking skills and personal capabilities

In this unit we will:

- make connections in reading
- identify and discuss some of the features used by writers
- begin to show an awareness of how a writer uses language for effect, for example humour
- adopt personal opinions and draw conclusions
- experiment with different styles of writing, using appropriate vocabulary.

Being creative

'I have seen landscapes, notably in the Mourne Mountains and southwards which under a particular light made me feel that at any moment a **giant** might raise his head over the next ridge.'

C S Lewis

 Task 1

In this task you will:

*   be creative and try to imagine yourself in a magical land, using these photographs to prompt you.

*   What does the land look like?
*   Who do you see?
*   What are you feeling?
*   What is going to happen?

One of the most famous stories written by C S Lewis is *The Lion, the Witch and the Wardrobe*. In this story, Aslan the lion takes Lucy and Susan Pevensie, two of the main characters, on a magical journey across the land of Narnia, on his back.

Task 2

In this task you will:

- discuss how the writer uses punctuation to increase the pace of the text
- discuss how the writer uses forms of the verbs to increase the pace of the text.

Read the description and imagine you are on the journey.

That ride was perhaps the most wonderful thing that happened to them in Narnia. Have you ever had a gallop on a horse? Think of that; then take away the heavy noise of the hoofs and the jingle of the bits and imagine instead the almost noiseless padding of the great paws. Then imagine instead of the black or grey or chestnut back of the horse the soft roughness of golden fur, and the mane flying back in the wind. And then imagine you are going about twice as fast as the fastest race horse. But this is a mount that doesn't need to be guided and never grows tired. He rushes on and on, never missing his footing, never hesitating, threading his way with perfect skill between tree trunks, jumping over bush and briar and smaller streams, wading the larger, swimming the largest of all. And you are riding not on a road nor in a park nor even on the downs, but right across Narnia, in spring, down solemn avenues of beech and across sunny glades of oak, through wild orchards of snow-white cherry trees, past roaring waterfalls and mossy rocks and echoing caverns, up windy slopes alight with gorse bushes, and across the shoulders of heathery mountains and along giddy ridges and down, down, down again into wild valleys and out into acres of blue flowers.

At the beginning of the novel, Narnia is a magical world hidden from everyone and covered in a permanent cloak of winter. The youngest member of the Pevensie family, Lucy, comes across the magical world of Narnia by accident, through the back of a wardrobe. In this extract she meets an unusual character called Mr Tumnus, a Faun.

Task 3

In this task you will:

- read the extract as a dialogue between the two characters, marking out where the two speak
- read or listen to others reading it, thinking about the contrast between human and non-human worlds.

What Lucy found there

'Good evening,' said Lucy. But the Faun was so busy picking up its parcels that at first it did not reply. When it had finished it made her a little bow.

'Good evening, good evening,' said the Faun. 'Excuse me – I don't want to be inquisitive – but should I be right in thinking that you are a Daughter of Eve?'

'My name's Lucy,' said she, not quite understanding him.

'But you are – forgive me – you are what they call a girl?' said the Faun.

'Of course I'm a girl,' said Lucy.

'You are in fact Human.'

'Of course I'm human,' said Lucy, still a little puzzled.

'To be sure, to be sure,' said the Faun. 'How stupid of me! But I've never seen a Son of Adam or a Daughter of Eve before. I am delighted. That is to say –' and then it stopped as if it was going to say something it had not intended but had remembered in time. 'Delighted, delighted,' it went on. 'Allow me to introduce myself. My name is Tumnus.'

'I am very pleased to meet you, Mr Tumnus,' said Lucy.

'And may I ask, O Lucy Daughter of Eve,' said Mr Tumnus, 'how have you come into Narnia?'

'Narnia? What's that?' said Lucy.

'This is the land of Narnia,' said the Faun, 'where we are now; all that lies between the lamp-post and the great castle of Cair Paravel on the eastern sea. And you – you have come from the wild woods of the west?'

'I – I got in through the wardrobe in the spare room,' said Lucy.

'Ah!' said Mr Tumnus in a rather melancholy voice, 'if only I had worked harder at geography when I was a little Faun, I should no doubt know all about those strange countries. It is too late now.'

'But they aren't countries at all,' said Lucy, almost laughing. 'It's only just back there – at least – I'm not sure. It is summer there.'

'Meanwhile,' said Mr Tumnus, 'it is winter in Narnia, and has been for ever so long, and we shall both catch cold if we stand here talking in the snow. Daughter of Eve from the far land of Spare Oom where eternal summer reigns around the bright city of War Drobe, how would it be if you came and had tea with me?'

'Thank you very much, Mr Tumnus,' said Lucy. 'But I was wondering whether I ought to be getting back.'

'It's only just round the corner,' said the Faun, 'and there'll be a roaring fire – and toast – and sardines – and cake.'

'Well, it's very kind of you,' said Lucy. 'But I shan't be able to stay long.'

'If you will take my arm, Daughter of Eve,' said Mr Tumnus, 'I shall be able to hold the umbrella over both of us. That's the way. Now – off we go.'

And so Lucy found herself walking through the wood arm in arm with this strange creature as if they had known one another all their lives.

They had not gone far before they came to a place where the ground became rough and there were rocks all about the little hills up and little hills down. At the bottom of one small valley Mr Tumnus turned suddenly aside as if he were going to walk straight into an unusually large rock, but at the last moment Lucy found he was leading her into the entrance of a cave. As soon as they were inside she found herself blinking in the light of a wood fire. Then Mr Tumnus stooped and took a flaming piece of wood out of the fire with a neat little pair of tongs, and lit a lamp. 'Now we shan't be long,' he said, and immediately put a kettle on.

1   The Faun and Lucy are from two different worlds and this causes some confusion at the beginning of their conversation. The Faun calls Lucy three different things. What are they? What do you understand by the third title?

2   The Faun misunderstands where Lucy has come from. Can you explain what mistake he makes?

3   Find out what you can about Narnia from the passage.

4   Although Lucy is in a fantasy world, it has elements of the world she has left. What are these?

Sentence level work

Think about the sentence, 'Daughter of Eve from the far land of Spare Oom where eternal summer reigns around the bright city of War Drobe, how would it be if you came and had tea with me?'

Create a question to address to someone else including:

- a personal title
- the name of a fictional country
- a description of that land and
- a request.

Ask the question in an exaggerated manner.

Fantasy fiction genre

Now that you have read an example of fantasy fiction, what do you think are the elements of a fantasy fiction text? Think about setting, types of characters, plot and themes.

These are some of the common text conventions of a **fantasy text**.

- **Setting**: there is some link between the real world and a fantasy world; often an everyday item is the portal, for example wardrobe/train station.
- **Characters**: a human comes in contact with the fairy world or gains fairy powers; supernatural characters have supernatural powers; humans have moral strength against these powers; characters usually have unusual names.
- **Plot**: as fantastic as possible – this is a very important feature and it dominates the others.
- **Climax**: there is a showdown or final battle of forces.
- **Themes**: conflict between good and evil; acquiring power; natural versus unnatural forces.
- **Language elements**: unusual names for people and places, cracking a code.

Another very popular series of fantasy books, written by an Irishman, are the Artemis Fowl novels by Eoin Colfer. In this section of the unit you will read and discuss extracts from the first book in the series, *Artemis Fowl*, and then look for comparisons with the C S Lewis extract.

Let's introduce the main characters first.

Artemis Fowl is a child prodigy, a brilliant criminal, a 12-year-old intent on restoring his family fortune by stealing fairy gold.

'He still retained a childlike belief in magic, tempered by an adult determination to exploit it.'

Holly Short, his enemy for most of the novel, is a leprechaun, actually a captain in the LEPrecon, Lower Elements Police reconnaissance department.

'It's better to stay inconspicuous and let the humans have their stereotypes.'

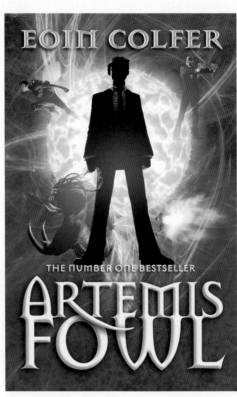

Step into magical places

  Task 4

In this task you will:

- read an extract from *Artemis Fowl* about the place where magic happens: Ireland
- be asked questions which prompt you to think about this country and Holly's view of it.

Finally the coast loomed ahead of her. The old country. Éiriú, the land where time began. The most magical place on the planet. It was here, 10,000 years ago, that the ancient fairy race, the Dé Danann, had battled against the demon Fomorians, carving the famous Giant's Causeway with the strength of their magical blasts. It was here that the Lia Fáil stood, the rock at the centre of the universe, where the fairy kings and later the human Ard Rí were crowned. And it was also here, unfortunately, that the Mud people were most in tune with magic, which resulted in a far higher people-sighting rate than you got anywhere else on the planet. Thankfully the rest of the world assumed that the Irish were crazy, a theory that the Irish themselves did nothing to debunk. They had got it into their heads that each fairy lugged around a pot of gold with them wherever they went. While it was true that LEP had a ransom fund, because of its officers' high-risk occupation, no human had ever taken a chunk of it yet. This didn't stop the Irish population in general from skulking around rainbows, hoping to win the supernatural lottery.

1   How many words are there for Ireland?

2   Text-mark the characteristics of the Irish according to Holly.

Task 5

This extract is from early in the novel when Artemis Fowl, the human, or Mud Person, captures Holly, the fairy. Butler works for Artemis, as his butler! As you read it, think about the features of fantasy fiction outlined earlier in the unit and find elements in this text.

Holly hooked the wings over a low branch, unstrapping the helmet to give her ears some air. You had to be careful with elfin ears – a few hours in the helmet and they started to flake. She gave the tips a massage. No dry skin there. That was because she had a daily moisturizing regime, not like some of the male LEP officers. When they took off their helmets, you'd swear it had just started to snow.

Holly paused for a minute to admire the view. Ireland certainly was picturesque. Even the Mud People hadn't been able to destroy that. Not yet anyway… Give them another century or two. The river was folding gently before her like a silver snake, hissing as the water tumbled across a stony bed. The oak tree crackled overhead, its branches rasping together in the bracing breeze.

Now, to work. She could do the tourist thing all night once her business was complete. A seed. She needed a seed. Holly bent to the ground, brushing the dried leaves and twigs from the clay's surface. Her fingers closed around a smooth acorn. That wasn't hard now, was it? she thought. All that remained for her to do was plant it somewhere else and her powers would come rushing back.

Butler checked the porta-radar, muting the volume in case the equipment betrayed their position. The red arm swept the screen with agonizing lethargy, and then… *Flash!* An upright figure by the tree. Too small for an adult, the wrong proportions for a child. He gave Artemis the thumbs-up. Possible match.

Artemis nodded, strapping the mirrored sunglasses across his brow. Butler followed his lead, popping the cap on his weapon's starlight scope. This was no ordinary dart rifle. It had been specially tooled for a Kenyan ivory hunter and had the range and rapid-fire capacity of a Kalashnikov. Butler had picked it up for a song from a government official after the ivory poacher's execution.

They crept into the night with

practised silence. The diminutive figure before them unhooked a contraption from around its shoulders and lifted a full-face helmet from a definitely non-human head. Butler wrapped the rifle strap twice around his wrist, pulling the stock into his shoulder.

He activated the scope and a red dot appeared in the centre of the figure's back. Artemis nodded and his manservant squeezed the trigger.

In spite of a million to one odds, it was at that precise moment that the figure bent low to the earth.

Something whizzed over Holly's head, something that glinted in the starlight. Holly had enough on-the-job experience to realize that she was under fire, and immediately curled her elfin frame into a ball, minimizing the target.

She drew her pistol, rolling towards the shelter of the tree trunk. Her brain scrambled for possibilities. Who could be shooting at her and why?

Something was waiting beside the tree. Something roughly the size of a mountain, but considerably more mobile.

'Nice pea-shooter,' grinned the figure, smothering Holly's gun hand in a turnip-sized fist.

Holly managed to extricate her fingers a nanosecond before they snapped like brittle spaghetti.

'I don't suppose you would consider peaceful surrender?' said a cold voice behind her.

Holly turned, elbows raised for combat.

'No,' sighed the boy melodramatically. 'I suppose not.'

Holly put on her best brave face.

'Stay back, human. You don't know what you're dealing with.'

The boy laughed. 'I believe, fairy, that you are the one unfamiliar with the facts.'

Fairy? He knew she was a fairy.

'I have magic mud-worm. Enough to turn you and your gorilla into pig droppings.'

The boy took a step closer. 'Brave words, miss. But lies nonetheless. If, as you say, you had magic, you would have no doubt used it by now. No, I suspect that you have gone too long without the Ritual and you are here to replenish your powers.'

Holly was dumbfounded. There was a human before her, casually spouting sacred secrets. This was disastrous. Catastrophic. It could mean the end of generations of peace. If the humans were aware of a fairy subculture, it was only a matter of time before the two species went to war. She must do something, and there was only one weapon left in her arsenal.

The *mesmer* is the lowest form of magic and requires only a trickle of power. There are even certain humans with a bent for the talent. It is the ability of even the most drained fairy to put a complete mind kibosh on any human alive.

Holly summoned the final dribble of magic from the base of her skull.

'Human,' she intoned, her voice suddenly resonating with bass tones, 'your will is mine.'

Artemis smiled, safe behind his mirrored lenses. 'I doubt it,' he said, and nodded curtly.

Holly felt the dart puncture the suit's toughened material, depositing its load of curare and succinylcholine chloride-based tranquillizer into her shoulder. The world instantly dissolved into a series of technicoloured bubbles and, try as she might, Holly couldn't seem to hold on to more than one thought. And that thought was: how did they know? It spiralled around her head as she sank into unconsciousness. How did they know? How did they know? How did they…

Artemis saw the pain in the creature's eyes as the hollow hypodermic plunged into her body. And for a moment he experienced misgivings. A female. He hadn't expected that. A female, like Juliet, or Mother. Then the moment passed and he was himself again.

'Good shooting,' he said, bending to study their prisoner. Definitely a girl. Pretty too. In a pointy sort of way.

'Sir?'

'Hmm?'

Butler was pointing to the creature's helmet. It was half-buried in a drift of leaves where the fairy had dropped it. A buzzing noise was coming from the crown.

Artemis picked up the contraption by the straps, searching for the source.

'Ah, here we are.' He plucked the viewcam from its slot, careful to point the lens away from him. 'Fairy technology. Most impressive,' he muttered, popping the battery from its groove. The camera whined and died. 'Nuclear power source, if I'm not mistaken. We must be careful not to underestimate our opponents.'

Butler nodded, sliding their captive into an oversized duffel bag. Something else to be lugged across two fields, a bog and a stile.

  Task 6

In this task you will:

- answer questions about the story and its characters and how it is written. Work as individuals or as a group.

1   Think about the **point of view** from which the story is told. What is the main point of view, the fairies or the Mud People? If you read it aloud you will be able to work out the different 'voices' more easily. If you can dramatise the story, then the sequence and overlap of the points of view will be more obvious.

2   As you read the extracts were you more sympathetic towards Holly or Artemis? Give your reasons.

3   Think about what you would expect a fairy's character to be like. What fairy qualities does Holly have? What human characteristics does she have? Give one piece of evidence for each from the passage.

4   Did you find the passages funny? If so, why? Think about characters, descriptions and unexpected details.

5   Look again closely at the three paragraphs at the beginning of the third section. Using text-marking or sequencing, think about the use of the word 'something'. Why did Eoin Colfer use it so often and what does it refer to?

The meeting between human and non-human

 **Task 7**

In this task you will:

- compare and contrast the two extracts from *The Lion, the Witch and the Wardrobe* and *Artemis Fowl*
- weigh up the pros and cons of different opinions
- use your knowledge of the features of fantasy fiction to structure your comparison.

1   Think back to the first activity in the unit, when you were visualising a magical landscape. Compare your landscapes with what you know about where the novels are set.

2   Compare the main characters, their qualities, situations and actions. Ask yourself questions about how the humans behaved compared with the non-humans; the girls compared with the boys.

3   Compare the way both stories are written. What was similar? What was different?

4   Which extract do you prefer and why?

A major theme in the genre of **fantasy fiction** is the battle between good and evil, and the climax of both these stories should not disappoint you.

If you enjoy this genre of writing, or these particular stories, why not go to your school library and get copies of these fantasy texts or others in the series?

What can you read next?

Other fantasy writers such as J K Rowling, Terry Pratchett, Philip Pullman, Debbi Gliori, Lewis Carroll, J R R Tolkien, Carlo Gebler and many more.

Step into fantasy: media reading

Computer games

Some of you are already fantasy fans through computer games and role playing games. Games such as those for *Harry Potter* and *Lord of the Rings* engage you, the player, with fantastic locations and narratives. You can take on the character of a wide range of creatures, from wizards to knights, and confront the forces of good and evil on each level. Think about, and discuss, how playing these games can lead you into this genre and influence how you respond as a reader.

Films

Have you seen a film or television adaptation of the C S Lewis books? Think about how the most recent film version of *The Lion, the Witch and the Wardrobe* (2006) uses computer technology to convey the magic.

  Task 8

In this task you will:

- read film or book reviews online.

Read the film review page on www.bullseyeonline.net/movies/NARNIA or

www.justpressplay.net/movies/reviews/127-The-Chronicles-of-Narnia .

For reviews of novels try www.readingmatters.co.uk . The reviews of *Artemis Fowl* are from far and wide. Why not add your own? Or visit www.fanfiction.net where you can post your own writing in the style of one of the authors.

 **Task 9**

In this task you will:

- search for information on the two Irish writers featured in this unit.
1 Search LNI library for information on C S Lewis and Eoin Colfer.
2 Select the information you find most interesting and save it on Myfiles.

Alternatively, use the school or local library for research.

Some starter points would include:

Date of birth

....

Place of birth

....

School

....

Most famous books

....

Date of birth

....

Place of birth

....

School

....

Most famous books

....

As part of your research into C S Lewis, find out about the places you can visit in Northern Ireland which have connections to the writer: the Mourne Mountains, St Mark's Church of Ireland in Belfast and The Searcher statue beside Holywood Road Library which was designed by Ross Wilson in tribute to the writer.

The Searcher statue by Ross Wilson

Task 10

In this task you will:

- write an extended piece of work.

Choose one of the following.

Creative writing

Write a piece of fantasy fiction using the themes and ideas suggested in the unit, or ideas of your own.

Review writing

Write a review of either the film version of the book *The Lion, the Witch and the Wardrobe*, or of the book itself. Alternatively, write a review of another fantasy text for example *Harry Potter*, *Lord of the Rings*.

Writing up research

Write a profile of a local writer which includes information about their life and their writing.

When making your choice consider which type of writing you prefer or at which you would like to improve.

Word bank

Here are some interesting words from this unit.

fantasy (n)	leprechaun (n)	The challenge is that you will be able to:
fantastic (adj)	stereotype (n and v)	
landscape (n)	diminutive (adj)	• spell them
melancholy (adj)	extricate (v)	• understand them
picturesque (adj)	catastrophic (adj)	• use them.

Unit review

Here we will:

- review your own work

- recognise your personal strengths and weaknesses.

Discuss these questions in pairs or small groups. Record your responses in your Writing Portfolio.

- Do you understand what is meant by 'fantasy fiction'?

- Do you feel more confident about using language for effect in written and spoken English?

- Can you compare and contrast similar texts?

- Have you found out about local writers, and developed your research skills?

- Do you feel more confident about expressing your views about writing?

Unit 2: No stranger here

What we will be doing

In this unit we will:

- investigate local dialect
- discuss poems
- research poets' lives and work
- work in groups
- write poetry
- compile a glossary
- create a class anthology.

What we will be learning

In this unit we will learn to:

- find out how a poet's social and cultural background influences his/her writing
- recognise and use personification, metaphor and strong adjectives
- recognise differences between dialect and Standard English.

Thinking skills and personal capabilities

In this unit we will:

- be creative
- solve problems
- work with others.

Local dialect and slang

  ## Task 1

In this task you will:

- listen actively and share opinions
- classify and compare information.

We use language every day. There are many varieties of a language. English is spoken in many parts of the world but it is spoken differently, even where it is the first language of the speaker.

Put this paragraph into your normal spoken language.

> The guy in the automobile broke his blinkers when he tried to back up in a narrow street and he knocked my garbage can off the sidewalk. He raced away but ran out of gas at the intersection. I used my cell phone to call the cops.

What country do you think the speaker is from?

Perhaps this paragraph is easier to understand.

> Wheesht your greetin'. You're a bonnie bairn and I dinna ken why ye let that crabbit cratur borrow your gutties. He's awa intae the hoose so stop your girnin'- ye'll just have to thole it.

Glossary

dialect: a variety of language used by people from a particular geographic area

slang: language particular to a particular group used to differentiate the group from society at large; slang words tend to go out of fashion after a time, for example, 'fab' gave way to 'cool' and then to 'wicked'

Some of these words are part of our **dialect**. Which ones do you recognise?

In pairs, discuss how many non-Standard English words you use in everyday speech. Then work in groups of four and find how many words and phrases you have in common.

Task 2

In this task you will:

- experiment with ideas
- seek advice when necessary.

Choose two or three of the dialect words you have discussed of which you like the sound. Put each in a sentence and illustrate the sentences.

What would you do with *dander*, *oxter* or *scaldie*?

  Task 3

In this task you will:

- give and respond to feedback
- make predictions and examine evidence.

The moon, as she hunkers here…

Speedwell *Leon McAuley*

I gulder to me da: 'Dinnae gut him wi your gully,
He's only a harmless crayter…'

Phemios & Medon *Michael Longley*

…'A right-looking night,'
he might say, 'I was dandering by
and says I, I might as well call.'

The Other Side *Seamus Heaney*

…the sweating happed-up self…

Ness Wood Nature Notes *Ann McKay*

In these extracts you can see that our local poets use dialect to express exactly what they see or feel. In pairs, rephrase these extracts and put them into Standard English. Which version do you prefer? Why?

 **Task 4**

In this task you will:

- organise and plan how to go about a task
- use your own and others' ideas to locate sources of information
- use a range of methods to collate, record and represent information
- use ICT.

There are many Ulster poets. Use the internet, an encyclopedia, or the library to find out more about local poets. Select one about whom you have enjoyed learning.

- Note his/her birthplace on a map of Ulster.
- Beside this, write his/her name, date of birth (and date of death, if applicable).
- Write these details in your portfolio.
- Make some notes on what you learned of the social, political and religious background of the poet. What was Ulster like when he/she was growing up?
- Write the titles of one or more volumes of this poet's work.
- Copy the words of one poem that you like into your portfolio.

Prepare a short presentation for your class, giving background information about the poet and including a reading of a poem written by him/her. Then respond to questions, posed by your classmates, about the poem.

The importance of location

Glossary

universal: able to be experienced by people anywhere in the world

 ## Task 5

In this task you will:

- focus and sustain attention
- experiment with ideas and language
- learn from, and value, other people's ideas.

Where we are born will influence the way that we write, and also what we write about. The themes of many poems are **universal**: themes such as love, hate, family, death and fear. Everyone can experience these. However, not everyone lives in Ulster, so poems written about particular Ulster places are special to this part of the world.

Patrick Kavanagh was brought up in the country, in County Monaghan. He writes about the townland of Shancoduff.

Shancoduff

My black hills have never seen the sun rising,
Eternally they look North towards Armagh.
Lot's wife would not be salt if she had been
Incurious as my black hills that are happy
When dawn whitens Glassdrummond chapel.

My hills hoard the bright shillings of March
While the sun searches in every pocket.
These are my Alps and I have climbed the Matterhorn
With a sheaf of hay for three perishing calves
In the field under the Big Forth of Rocksavage.

The sleety winds fondle the rushy beards of Shancoduff
While the cattle-drovers sheltering in the Featherna Bush
Look up and say: 'Who owns them hungry hills
That the water-hen and snipe have forsaken?
A poet? Then by heavens he must be poor.'
I hear and is my heart not badly shaken?

Patrick Kavanagh

1   Note in your portfolio any examples of **personification** or **metaphor** used in this poem.

2   What are the poet's feelings about his townland?

Glossary

personification: when a writer makes a thing act like a person
metaphor: when a writer says something *is* something else

Louis MacNeice was a city dweller.

Carrickfergus (extract)

I was born in Belfast between the mountain and the gantries
To the hooting of lost sirens and the clang of trams:
Thence to smoky Carrick in County Antrim
Where the bottle-neck harbour collects the mud which jams

The little boats beneath the Norman castle,
The pier shining with lumps of crystal salt;
The Scotch Quarter was a line of residential houses
But the Irish Quarter was a slum for the blind and halt.

The brook ran yellow from the factory stinking of chlorine,
The yarn-mill called its funeral cry at noon;
Our lights looked over the lough to the lights of Bangor
Under the peacock aura of a drowning moon.

Louis MacNeice

1   Do you learn much about the poet's feelings in this poem?
2   Consider the adjectives MacNeice uses in this poem. What impression do they give of Carrickfergus?

Maura Johnston is from the townland of Mowillian in County Derry. Here she notes the changes that have taken place in that townland.

Mowillian

Somewhere along the line
The loanin turned into a lane
And the jamb wall disappeared.
A new villa rose on the old
Thorn's mangled site, bold
On the hillside, wonderfully pared.

The boor trees' blooms are frittered.
The corncrake no longer patterns
The sweep of long, sweet summers.
And yet, yet still the small moss
Cheeper haunts the walled
Slopes, a brave unfettered cantor.

The forth, too, stands; a nest of trees
Cradling the seasons' certainties.

Maura Johnston

1　Can you find any dialect words in this poem?
2　What words or phrases do you like? Give reasons.
3　How does the poet feel about her townland?

Write about a place that is special for you. Use **imagery** such as personification to make your place come alive for the reader. Use adjectives and, if you like, dialect words if you think they will help describe the place.

Task 6

In this task you will:

- generate possible solutions
- listen actively and share opinions
- make predictions and examine evidence
- make ideas real by experimenting with language.

A poet who loved County Tyrone, and who wrote in the rhythms of Tyrone speech, was the Reverend W F Marshall. Here is one of his poems.

The Lad

They were no great aff-set anywhere,
The scutchers times ago,
For the drink it follyd the most of them
That wrought among the tow.
Plenishment they'd have little or noan
Except for what they'd stale,
And they'd make the childher go out an' beg
Gowpins of oaten male.

I knowed a scutcher that wrought in Shane,
He was a drunken scrub,
But he rared a son, an' I mind the son
A smart wee lump of a cub.
His clo'es were wings, an' his cap was tore,
An' his fire was the fire at the kill,
An' he went to school on his wee bare feet,
An' niver got half his fill.

Above the mill was a quare big hill,
He could see to the graveyard wall,
To the market-house an' the station gates,
An' the new Hibernian Hall.
You'd hear him singin' goan up the hill,
But the dear knows why he sung,
For the people thought they would see the day
When his da would sure be hung.

When the Twelfth was near he'd march the road,
His drumsticks in his han',
Boys, he was prime at the double rowl
On the lid of an oul' tin can.
He played his lone, for the other folk
Were ashamed of him an' his rags,
So he thrinneld his hoop an' waded the burn
An' ginneld for spricklybags.

I mind the year he took up with me,
The ploughin' had just begun,
I'd watch him leadin' the horses roun',
The dhrunken scutcher's son!
Little I thought that afterwards
More than a son he'd be,
For his father died in a water-shough
An' he come to live with me.

He was odd in a way; I think he heerd
What nobody else could hear,
An' he seen what I could never see,
The more my sight was clear.
The top of a hill bewitched him still,
An' the flame at the mountain's rim,
But a runnin' burn was the best of all
For he sayed it sung to him.

There were some that went that far as to say
He was sure to turn out wil',
But the wee lad grew till he grew man big
An' kep the heart of a chile.
The longer he lived about the place
The less I had to fear.
There was never a word from him to me
But done me good to hear.

I'm feelin' oul since he went away,
An' my sight is gettin' dim;
I niver axed for to keep him back
When they needed men like him.
He's sleepin' now where the poppies grow,
In the coat that the bullets tore,
And what's a wheen of medals to me
When my own wee lad's no more.

Rev W F Marshall

In groups, discuss the language of this poem. Is much of it in dialect? How else would you describe the language of *The Lad*?

This is, in a sense, a narrative poem, about local events. Write a poem of your own, with a local setting. Use local speech patterns where you feel that is appropriate.

 **Task 7**

In this task you will:

- organise and plan how to go about a task
- sequence, order and classify
- take personal responsibility for working with others and evaluate your own contribution to the group
- use ICT.

Now that you have read poems by local poets and have written poems of your own, you are ready to collect these together. Work in groups of three. Each group will select at least one poem written by a member of your group and one poem written by a published Ulster writer. Prepare these for a class anthology by researching as much as you can about the writers and the poems.

The class anthology will be filmed. One member of the group will introduce the poet, one the poem and the final group member will read or recite the poem.

Word bank

Here are some interesting words from this unit.

poem (n)	metaphor (n)	The challenge is that you will be able to:
universal (adj)	personification (n)	• spell them
language (n)	imagery (n)	• understand them
dialect (n)	anthology (n)	• use them.
simile (n)		

Unit review

Here we will:

- be aware of personal strengths and limitations
- review learning and some aspects that might be improved.

How well did you:

- identify what you needed to know
- use research skills
- recognise and understand the use of dialect
- work with others
- use imagery in poems
- use dialect and imagery in your own writing?

Which area do you feel needs more practice?

Unit 3: Reading film

What we will be doing

In this unit we will:

- talk and write about film
- write a film review
- come up with ideas for your own film and 'pitch' it to the rest of your class
- design a storyboard
- choose music and sound effects for your film
- use ICT to design a film poster.

What we will be learning

In this unit we will learn to:

- recognise different film genres
- understand how films are aimed at different audiences
- identify how film narratives are structured
- create a storyboard
- 'read' a film, identifying shot types and their effects
- recognise how film posters are used to target and attract audiences.

Thinking skills and personal capabilities

In this unit we will:

- distinguish between fact and opinion
- listen actively and share opinions
- organise and plan how to go about a task
- experiment with designs and outcomes
- communicate with a sense of audience and purpose.

Film and you

 ## Task 1

In this task you will:

- discuss your experiences of watching film with others.

Work with a partner and answer these questions.

1 What is your favourite film?
2 What type of films do you enjoy watching?
3 Who are your favourite actors?
4 How do you find out about new films?
5 Where do you watch films?

Task 2

In this task you will:

- discuss and classify the films that you watch.

There are many different types of film; the term used to describe a 'type' of film is **genre**.

Here are some different film genres. Can you add to the list?

- Action/adventure
- Comedy
- Horror
- Romance

1. In pairs, discuss the last three films you watched and identify their genre.

2. How did you know what genre they were?

Reading a **review** of a film can help you decide if you want to see it.

Pirates of the Caribbean 3: At World's End
Starring: Johnny Depp, Keira Knightley, Orlando Bloom
Director: Gore Verbinski
Certificate: 12

CLUTCHING a mast swaying high over the crashing ocean, Captain Jack Sparrow and Davy Jones fight to the death in an awe-inspiring climax to one of the most popular trilogies in movie history.

It's a movie packed with thrills, spills and chills, every cent of its gigantic $150million budget put to stunning use.

Following on from last year's *Dead Man's Chest*, these are dark times for the Age of Piracy. With loveable buccaneer Jack (Depp) missing presumed dead, the evil East India Company now controls the waves with the malevolent Davy Jones (Bill Nighy) roaming the world's oceans in his ghost ship, The Flying Dutchman.

As tyranny prevails on the high seas, it's up to young lovers Will Turner and Elizabeth Swann (Orlando Bloom and Keira Knightley) to save piracy from a watery grave by gathering together the Nine Lords of the Brethren Court.

But one of the lords is missing. Jack is trapped in Davy Jones' Locker – his own personal hell, a desert without a drop of seawater – following his terrifying encounter with a monstrous kraken in the last movie.

It means Will and Elizabeth must embark on a dangerous mission to find the charts and a ship that will lead them to their salty seadog friend.

But neither has reckoned with Oriental pirate Captain Sao Feng (Chow Yun-Fat, of *Crouching Tiger* fame) who's slipperier than a barrel of eels.

Everyone who enjoyed *Dead Man's Chest* will be hooked by this three-quel which, like the earlier film, is crammed to bursting with multiple plots, seafaring showdowns and spectacular special effects.

Once again, Depp proves to be a natural-born swashbuckler, flaying his hands around and delivering his humorous lines in Jack's trademark slur.

But while *At World's End* is sure to drum up a treasure trove of box-office booty for Disney, it's unlikely to win new converts. Once again director Gore Verbinski has overburdened proceedings with too many plotlines (15, including Barbossa's return from the dead), too many baddies and just too much action.

With so many special effects they start to lose the wow factor as the movie goes on. And, believe me, this is a film that goes on, clocking in at no less than 168 minutes. Pirates may make your jaw thud to the ground, but it'll also make your bum go blue.

But they're unlikely to prevent Pirates launching a fresh assault on our pockets. Shot back-to-back with the second part during a gruelling 284-day shoot, there's already talk of a fourth film. Pirates' legion of fans worldwide will no doubt be yo-ho-hoping Captain Jack will be sailing again.

Task 3

In this task you will:

- examine evidence
- distinguish fact from opinion
- learn about the features of a film review.

1   Is *Pirates of the Caribbean* a romance, a comedy or an action-adventure film?

2   List two positive and two negative comments made about the film.

3   Why do you think this review is written in the present tense?

4   How does the writer address the reader?

5   What do you notice about the **style of the writing** in this review? For instance the language is informal.

6   Reviews are a mixture of **fact** and **opinion**. Copy the table and make a note of some of the **facts** and **opinions** in the review.

Fact	Opinion
The film cost 150 million dollars	*Everyone who enjoyed Dead Man's Chest will be hooked by this three-quel*

7   What did you discover about how facts and opinions are used in this review?

8   What are the features of a good film review? Use this and other reviews to help you decide. Make a list of features and share it with the rest of your class.

 **Task 4**

In this task you will:

- plan and write a film review.

Choose a film you have recently watched and write a review of it for a teen magazine. Include details on:

- the title
- genre
- plot
- characters
- any special effects/features
- your opinions on the above.

What's the story?

Most film narratives (storylines) contain five main stages.

1	**Exposition**	Introduction to the setting and characters.
2	**Development**	You learn more about the characters.
3	**Complication**	Something happens to disrupt the lives of the characters.
4	**Conflict**	The characters are at odds with someone or something.
5	**Resolution**	The problem is overcome and order is restored.

 **Task 5**

In this task you will:

- sequence and classify information.

Here is a summary of the plot of *Stuart Little*; however, it is muddled up.

- The family cat, Snowball, arranges for Stuart to be taken far away from home.
- Snowball feels sorry for Stuart and helps him find his way home. Once there he is reunited with his family.
- Stuart comes up against the family cat.
- The Littles are introduced.
- They adopt Stuart, a mouse!

Organise it using the five stages of narrative. For example,

1 Exposition: The Littles are introduced
2 Development

Choose a film you have recently watched; try to organise the storyline into the five features of narrative. Share your findings with the rest of the class.

Are there certain types of films that are more difficult to fit into this pattern? What types of film are they?

The big idea

 ## Task 6

In this task you will:

- experiment with ideas.

Have you got any good ideas for a new film? Produce a **concept map** of your ideas and include details on:

- the genre of your film
- the setting
- the characters
- some essential props.

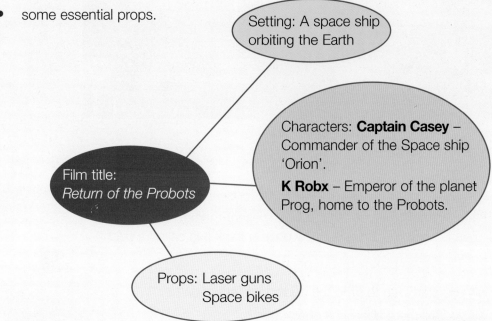

Setting: A space ship orbiting the Earth

Characters: **Captain Casey** – Commander of the Space ship 'Orion'.

K Robx – Emperor of the planet Prog, home to the Probots.

Film title: *Return of the Probots*

Props: Laser guns Space bikes

Narrative

Exposition: *Orion is on a routine mission to Mars.*

Development: *We learn that many years ago Captain Casey's family were destroyed in an attack on planet Earth by the Probots, from the planet Prog. He swore he would avenge their deaths.*

Complication: *An enemy ship is detected on Orion's radar; it appears to be a ship belonging to the Probots.*

Conflict: *The Probots are on a mission to…*

Task 7

In this task you will:

- give and respond to feedback.

Once you have planned your ideas for a film, present them to the rest of your class. This is known as a **pitch**. Why do you think it is called a pitch?

Points to consider when planning your pitch.

- What will you start with to grab the audience's attention?
- What will you tell them about the characters?
- What actors do you think would be effective in these roles?
- What will you reveal about the narrative?
- Try not to simply **recount** your ideas but build an image of the scenes in your listener's mind.

Afterwards ask their opinions on whether they think people will want to see this film.

Planning with pictures

Storyboarding is a very important part of making a film. Before a film is made, a storyboard of images is produced. A storyboard helps you to plan each scene, what it should look like and where the camera should be.

Notice how various different types of **shots** are used to make the film interesting. However, there are other reasons for using different types of shots.

Extreme close-up: This is a very close up shot of your subject. This is a very intimate shot and can be used to make the viewer feel quite uncomfortable.

Close-up: This is where the subject's head and shoulders fill the screen. It is used to show emotion or create intimacy.

Medium shot: This is used to show the subject's upper body as well as some background detail.

Long shot: This is used to show a broad view of a place. Films often open on long shots to let the audience know where and when the story is set.

- Can you think of any other types of shots you have seen used in films?
- Find out what they are called and think about their effect on the viewer.

Task 8

In this task you will:

- watch an extract from a film, identify the shot types used and discuss why they may have been used.

Watch the opening 10–20 seconds of any film. Watch it several times. Can you identify the different types of shots used? Consider why each shot was framed in this way. Share your ideas with the rest of your class.

 Task 9

In this task you will:

- experiment with ideas.

Storyboard the opening sequence of the film that you pitched to your class in Task 7. Your storyboard should consist of between 12 and 16 frames.

Before you begin, consider these questions.

- What will happen in the first few seconds of your film?
- What are the best types of shots to show this?
- What other information will you need to include in your storyboard?

Sounds good

Music, dialogue, sound effects and voice-overs are all commonly used in films.

   Task 10

In this task you will:

- examine options
- listen actively and share opinions.

Watch a sequence from a film and make notes on all the different sounds that you hear.

Work in groups.

1   What do you notice about when **music** is used?
2   Was the music coming from the **world of the film** or was it added over the film?
3   Was a **voice-over** used? If so, explain why.

4 Were any **sound effects** used?

5 Experiment by adding different music, voice-overs and sound effects to the sequence. What happens?

6 What music would you never hear used in a horror movie? What music would you never hear used in a comedy?

7 Make a note of what you have learned about how and why sound is used in films. Share your findings with the rest of the class.

 Task 11

In this task you will:

● experiment with ideas.

When you drew your storyboard you were considering what the audience would **see**. You also need to consider what they will **hear**.

Return to your storyboard and consider what the audience will hear in the opening few seconds of your film. What dialogue, music, sound effects or voice-over will you include? Make notes on your storyboard.

Picture this...

 Task 12

In this task you will:

- consider how films are promoted.

Once a film is made, the general public need to be made aware that it is about to be released. In **pairs,** make a note of the different ways you find out about new films.

Film posters are an important way of making the public aware of a new film. They are carefully designed to appeal to the film's **target audience** and to tell them as much information as possible about the film itself.

Task 13

In this task you will:

- examine evidence and make predictions.

In pairs look carefully at the posters. Identify these parts.

- Title
- Images
- Graphics
- Typography
- Star names
- Tag line

Now consider these questions.

1 Can you tell the film's **genre** from the poster? Explain how.
2 What do you learn about the film from looking at the poster?
3 Who is the **target audience** for these posters? Explain how you know this.
4 What are the most **persuasive** features of the film poster?

 Task 14

In this task you will:
- experiment with ideas
- communicate with a sense of audience and purpose.

Design a poster for your film. Make sure you include these details:

- the title of the film
- details of who stars in it
- graphics /images from the film
- a tag line
- release date
- website address.

Think about it
Before you produce your poster make notes on the following.

- What is the **function** of this poster?
- Who is the **target audience** for your film?
- How will your poster **appeal** to them?

Word bank

Here are some interesting words from this unit.

exposition (n)	pitch (n)	The challenge is that you will be able to:
props (n)	tag line (n)	• spell them
target audience (n)	resolution (n)	• understand them
complication (n)	dialogue (n)	• use them.

Unit review

Here we will:

- review your own work

- recognise your strengths and weaknesses.

Discuss these questions in pairs, or write your responses in your Writing Portfolio.

- How can you identify a film's genre?

- What are the features of a good film review?

- What are some of the main stages of a film narrative?

- What is a pitch?

- What is a storyboard? Who uses them and why?

- Can you list various shot types? Do you know why they are used and what effect they have on the viewer?

- What types of sound can be added to a film? How does this add to how we understand the film?

- What are some of the typical features of a film poster?

Unit 4: Just a minute, let me explain...

What we will be doing

In this unit we will:

- talk (in pairs and in groups) to question and develop thinking about complex issues
- carry out problem-solving activities – barrier games
- give a commentary to link words with images
- use ICT to view, research and present work.

What we will be learning

In this unit we will learn to:

- recognise the structure and features of explanations
- use clear and concise language when explaining how or why something works or happens
- summarise the main points in a discussion and explain the conclusions of the group
- plan and deliver explanations to an audience
- use connectives when explaining something.

Thinking skills and personal capabilities

In this unit we will:

- listen actively to others and ask focused questions
- give and respond to feedback
- use your own and others' ideas to locate sources of information
- make sense of information by making links between cause and effect
- organise and plan how to go about a task
- review learning and identify some aspect that might be improved.

Identifying explanation texts

 **Task 1**

In this task you will:

- listen actively and share opinions with your peers.

1 **Why** do we need to explain things?

2 **What** kinds of things need to be explained?

3 **Who** do you think might need to use explanation as an essential part of their job? List some examples.

4 Choose one person from your list and explain clearly why it is necessary for this person to explain things in their work. Share examples with your class.

5 **What** do you consider to be important when explaining something to someone else?

 **Task 2**

In this task you will:

- compare and evaluate information.

Read these texts.

Using the photocopier

Turn on the red switch.

Wait for the green light to show.

Put your master sheet under the top flap (face down).

Press the green light.

Wait a few seconds.

Take your copy from the side tray (right hand side).

Lift up the top flap and remove your master sheet.

Turn off the red switch.

What is global warming?

Global warming means the increased heating of the atmosphere caused by human activities. World temperatures are estimated to have risen by 0.5°C in the 20th century and could rise by up to 5.8°C by the end of the 21st century. A 1°C rise in world temperatures could mean significant melting of the polar ice caps, worldwide rises in sea level and serious damage to existing ecosystems.

Causes of global warming

Global warming is caused by greenhouse gases which trap heat in the atmosphere; the main greenhouse gases are carbon dioxide, nitrogen dioxide and methane. Carbon dioxide is responsible for 50% of global warming.

Effects of global warming

Sea levels could rise by up to 1.5 metres because the sea expands as it is heated: also ice caps at the poles and glaciers could melt leading to sea levels rising by up to 5 metres. As a result of this, many low-lying areas could suffer from devastating floods. Tourism, in particular skiing, could also be affected in places such as the Alps and even the Scottish Highlands due to less snow because of rising temperatures.

Further, the effect on humans could be dramatic. The increasingly hot temperatures can injure people with heart problems because their cardiovascular systems will have to work harder. Hot conditions can also spread pests and diseases and attack crops. The effects will vary by region, over time, and will depend on each of us to adapt to or cope with the change.

Adapted from Geography for CCEA GCSE, *Kay Clarke, Linda Francis, Petula Henderson, Cormac McKinney*

Note

Explanation texts generally answer the questions how and why.

In pairs, discuss what you think the **difference** is between the two texts and use the chart to record the **key features** about each text type.

Make sure that you state the genre of each text.

Reminder of the six main non-fiction genre or text types.

Recount

Report

Procedural

Explanation

Exposition

Argument/discussion

Main features of each text

Photocopier Genre Procedure	Global warming Genre Explanation
a series of sequenced steps written in imperative	

Recognising features of explanation texts

Task 3

In this task you will:

- read an explanation which explains how something works
- answer the questions.

The water cycle

Most of us take water for granted. We turn on the tap and out it pours. However, if you travel to hotter countries such as Africa or India, you will know that water is a precious commodity and one that gives life or death.

Although vast areas of water cover the world, only 1% is drinkable – the rest is seawater. This small amount of fresh water keeps living creatures and plants alive. Luckily, it is constantly recycled through 'the water cycle'.

Here is how it works.

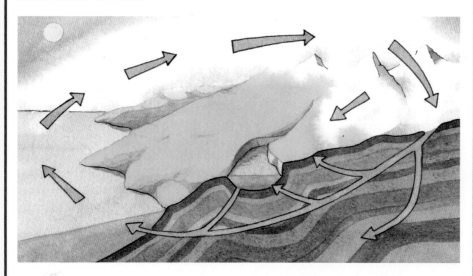

The heat from the sun blasts down at the earth. This heat evaporates some of the water from the oceans, ponds and rivers then the evaporated water rises as 'water vapour'. As the water vapour rises upwards it gets colder and condenses into droplets of water.

In the upper atmosphere, billions of these tiny droplets join together to form clouds – the more droplets that form together, the heavier the clouds become until they can hold no more. Eventually the weight and pressure causes the larger droplets to fall – as rain or snow. So, down it falls, back into the oceans, lakes, ponds and rivers.

This miraculous process is continually happening without us being aware of it. It is nature's very own recycling process. Nothing is wasted! Perhaps we should be like nature – don't waste water. It is precious.

Adapted from Badger Key Stage 3
Literacy Starters

1 How can you tell this is an explanation text?
2 What do you notice about the layout?
3 What is the function of each paragraph?
4 What tense is the text written in?
5 Write down three connectives which signal **time**.
6 Write down three **causal** connectives.
7 The **dash** is used four times. What purpose does it serve?

Task 4

In this task you will:

- work in pairs
- think creatively
- research information.

1 Think of an unusual or interesting gadget and be prepared to explain exactly what it is, what it is used for or how it works (without actually naming it). You can research necessary information using ICT if you wish.

- Write down your explanation.
- Now explain in detail (to a partner or to the class group) exactly how it works or what it does.
- Your partner or the other students should try to guess what it is from your detailed explanation.
- You can prompt each other by asking questions if an explanation is not clear.
- Suggest what would have helped to make the explanation clearer.

2 How good do you think you are at explaining things?

Write some of the **key features** you need to remember when explaining something in a copy of this grid.

Key features of explanation texts

Task 5

In this task you will:

- explain ICT processes to an adult who is not ICT literate.

Explain (with or without visuals) either

- the process of downloading an MP3 file from the internet onto your iPod or MP3 player

or

- how you would download a computer game/MP4 file from the internet onto your PSP.

Try this activity in groups of three. Student one explains, student two listens and student three observes. (The observer is then asked to assess or comment on the effectiveness of the explanation.)

The observer should use the key features of explanation texts noted in Task 4 to assess talk. Here are some examples to consider.

- Was the language used clear and concise?
- Was the technical language explained?
- Was each step sufficiently explained answering how or why something happened?
- Were connectives used to make the explanation easy to follow?

Task 6

In this task you will:

- examine evidence
- distinguish fact from opinion
- consider issues regarding **sustainable development**.

First, consider these issues in pairs.

1   Do you feel that you are doing enough to protect and conserve the environment?

2   Discuss some of the things that we all could do to sustain the current environment.

3   Suggest things that we must not do if we are to ensure sustainable development in Northern Ireland.

4   Look closely at these pictures. They are referred to as Ecological Footprints. What do you think that they are saying?

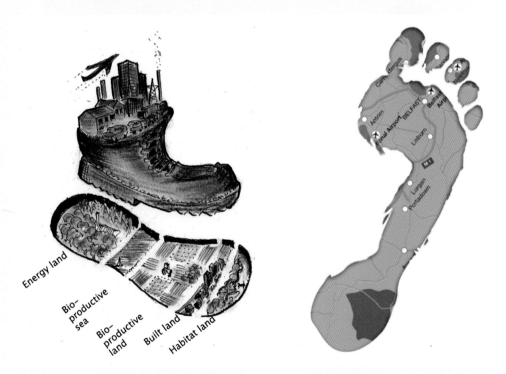

5   Read this explanation and then, in pairs or small groups, share, and perhaps add to, your explanation of the footprints from Question 4.

What are Ecological Footprints?

Ecological footprints demonstrate how our use of resources impact on the environment. Everyone, from an individual to a whole city or country, has an impact on the Earth. This is because we consume the products and services of nature.

The ecological footprint approach uses land as its currency and provides a notional figure for the land required to support an individual, a school or a nation's population at its present standard of living.

If all the biologically productive land and sea on the planet is divided by the number of people inhabiting it, the result is a statistical average of 2.2 hectares per person.

Recent studies, however, estimate the average Earth share to be 1.87 hectares.

The Earth share can be considered to be the maximum footprint allowance for each of us, without depriving either future generations or those now living in other regions of the world.

Why measure our ecological footprint?

Once an ecological footprint has been calculated, it can be used as an indicator to show trends over time and to make comparisons between countries, regions and even individuals. The data can also be used to examine the impact we have on the footprint (e.g. waste management, sustainable transport measures, renewable energy production). Governments and even schools can then develop and prioritise strategies which help to reduce the footprint.

Adapted from Lines from the Environmental Education Forum, *September 2004*

6   Make an ecological footprint for yourself in your own school or area by doing a short quiz with fifteen easy questions. Research this information on www.earthday.net/footprint/index.asp

This footprint quiz estimates how much productive land and water you use and what you discard. After answering the fifteen questions, you will be able to compare your footprint to that of other people and to what is available on the planet.

Information relating to Northern Ireland is available on this website:

www.northern-limits.com

Caution!

> This quiz might surprise you, shock you or even make you think!
> However, remain calm, but not too calm. Take action!

Glossary

form: a particular format or layout to express your ideas for example, speech, *PowerPoint*, poster

7　Are you happy with what your footprint is saying? Give your reasons.

8　Consider in pairs how to *reduce your footprints*.

9　Outline your suggestions and choose a particular **form** to explain your thoughts to others in your class.

Planning and producing explanation texts

  Task 7

In this task you will:

- use ideas from your group to locate sources of information
- break tasks into subtasks and develop a plan of action.

In groups of four or five consider this question and begin to plan your action.

How could you make your school more eco-friendly?

You might find this website useful: www.jointhebiggerpicture.co.uk.

You can discover your own carbon footprint. You can compare it with your friends and then decide what you can do to improve it and the environment!

If you need some ideas, you can click on the words: *reduce*, *recycle* and *reconsider* on this website for ideas about how you might make your environment more eco-friendly.

In this task, remember to consider

- your purpose and audience
- your methodology (planning)
- the form of your presentation (for example *PowerPoint*, speech, flyer, pamphlet)
- where it will be presented (for example school website).

When you are ready deliver your ideas to the class. Support your work with visuals, images or graphs, as appropriate to the task.

Task 8

In this task you will:

- explain a plan or process to your group.

Explain to the rest of your class either

- how you planned and put together your presentation, indicating any problems or issues that you faced

or

- a particular process in detail, for example how you used digital images as a background or how you created a slide show or storyboard.

Here is an extract from one Year 9 student who explained in detail how to import photographs into a *PowerPoint* presentation. Perhaps you can use this as a guide!

Importing photographs into PowerPoint

If text is not required on a slide, choose a blank layout when inserting pictures. Your pictures can be resized by grabbing one of the handles in the corners of the picture and dragging it backwards and forwards to suit your purpose.

Many modern digital cameras take pictures at a very high resolution – typically between 2 and 5 mega pixels, but this level of resolution is simply not necessary in a slide presentation. When pictures at this resolution are embedded within a PowerPoint presentation, this can produce a huge unmanageable file.

However, do not worry! PowerPoint has a quick and easy fix for this. Before a presentation is saved, it allows all photographs to be 'compressed'. This reduces the size of the file considerably and makes it run more efficiently. Good luck!

Word bank

Here are some interesting words from this unit.

explanation (n)	moreover (adv)	The challenge is that you will be able to:
ecological (adj)	subsequently (adv)	
renewable (adj)	connectives (n)	• spell them
explain (v)	consequently (adv)	• understand them
energy (n)	despite (prep)	• use them.
strategies (n)	nevertheless (adv)	
sustainable (adj)	therefore (adv)	
recycle (v)	meanwhile (adv)	
development (n)		

Unit review

Here we will:

- review your own work

- recognise your personal strengths and weaknesses.

In this unit, how well did you:

- recognise and understand the difference between procedural texts and explanation texts

- use research skills

- solve problems

- work with others

- organise and plan your explanations

- deliver your final explanation to the class (did you include the key features discussed and noted down in your grid)?

Unit 5: Star-cross'd lovers

What we will be doing

In this unit we will:

- read extracts from *Romeo and Juliet*
- participate in a range of drama activities
- explore and respond to the play and its characters
- talk and write about the play and its themes.

What we will be learning

In this unit we will learn:

- about the plot of *Romeo and Juliet*
- how Shakespeare uses language in the play for particular effect
- how themes explored in the play are still relevant to audiences today
- how to develop and sustain a role.

Thinking skills and personal capabilities

In this unit we will:

- make links between cause and effect
- understand how actions and words affect others
- organise and plan how to go about a task
- make new connections between ideas and information
- ask focused questions.

Task 1

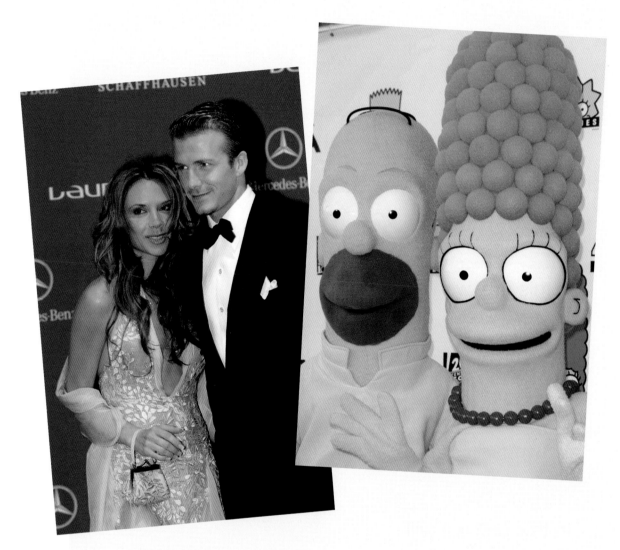

In this task you will:

- listen and share opinions.

1 In pairs, describe the qualities your perfect partner would have.

2 If your parents were to choose a perfect partner for you, would they choose the same qualities?

3 How important is it to you that your parents approve of your choice of partner?

The Montagues versus the Capulets

Task 2

Act 1 Scene 1

In this task you will:

- examine evidence and work in groups to perform a scene from the play.

Verona's streets

The Capulet servants, Gregory and Sampson, are talking in the street. Two Montague servants, Abraham and Balthasar, come by.

Gregory: Here comes two of the house of Montagues.

Sampson: My naked weapon is out. Quarrel: I will back thee.

Gregory: I will frown as they pass by and let them take it as they list.

Sampson: Nay, as they dare. I will bite my thumb at them; which is disgrace to them if they bear it.

Sampson aims this insulting gesture at the Montague servants who cannot ignore it.

Abraham: Do you bite your thumb at us, sir?

Sampson: I do bite my thumb, sir.

Abraham: Do you bite your thumb at us, sir?

Gregory: Do you quarrel, sir?

Abraham: Quarrel, sir? No, sir.

> **Sampson:** But if you do, sir, I am for you. I serve as good a man as you. Draw if you be men. Gregory, remember thy swashing blow.
>
> *A fight breaks out.*

1 In groups, read through the scene and discuss what you think is happening. Make notes on **two things** you know and **one thing** you would like to know more about.

2 In your groups discuss and make notes on these.

Movement

- How should the characters move?
- How close do they get to each other?
- What gestures will they use?

Language

- What tone should they use?
- Does their tone change? If so, where?
- At what pace should the lines be delivered?

---

3 Using your notes, experiment with acting out this scene and then present it to the rest of your group.

4 What have you learned about the Montagues and the Capulets from this scene?

5 Why do you think Shakespeare included a fight scene at the very start of this play?

The Prince of Verona, Prince Escalus, arrives just as the fight ends and makes this speech.

Rebellious subjects, enemies to peace,

Profaners of this **neighbour-stained steel**,—

Will they not hear? What, ho! you men, you beasts

…Throw your **mistempered** weapons to the ground,

And hear the sentence of your moved prince.

Three **civil brawls**, bred of an **airy** word,

By thee, old Capulet, and Montague,

Have thrice disturb'd the quiet of our streets,

…If ever you disturb our streets again,

Your lives shall pay the **forfeit** of the peace.

For this time, all the rest depart away.

Glossary

profaners: abusers
neighbour-stained steel: stained with the blood of their neighbours
mistempered: disorderly
civil brawls: street fights
airy: not serious; casual
forfeit: to lose the right to have

Task 3

In this task you will:

- examine evidence and plan a task.

1   How does the Prince refer to the men who have been fighting?

2   How do we know this is not the first time the Capulets and Montagues have fought on the streets of Verona?

3   What started these fights?

4   How will they pay if they 'disturb the streets' again?

5   Work with a partner and shorten each line of the speech into one or two words.

6   Practise presenting the shortened version. What are the key points the Prince wants to make?

7   Imagine you are one of the citizens of Verona who was present when the fight between the Montagues and the Capulets took place. Write a letter to a friend telling them what you witnessed.

Letters use the features of **recounts**.

Remember **recounts** should:

- be written in the past tense
- be written in chronological order
- use connectives.

Romeo

Romeo belongs to the Montague family. He was not present at the fight. He has other things on his mind. You overhear some of his comments as he talks to his friend Benvolio.

Out of her favour where I am in love.

I have lost myself… this is not Romeo.

Ay me! sad hours seem long.

Oh teach me how I should forget to think! (of Rosaline)

Griefs of mine own lie heavy in my breast,

O brawling love, O loving hate,

Task 4

In this task you will:

- experiment with ideas and questions.

In pairs, discuss these questions.

1 What do these comments tell you about how Romeo is feeling?
2 Why might he feel this way?
3 If you were Benvolio, what advice would you give Romeo?

In pairs, work together and present a role play of Benvolio giving Romeo advice.

The ball

Romeo is in love with a girl called Rosaline. He discovers she will be attending a ball at the house of his father's great enemy, Lord Capulet. He and his friends decide to go. Once there he sees a beautiful girl; however, it is not Rosaline, it is Juliet.

Romeo:

O, she doth teach the torches to burn bright!
It seems she hangs upon the cheek of night
As a rich jewel in an Ethiop's ear –

Beauty too rich for use, for earth too dear!
So shows a snowy dove trooping with crows,
As yonder lady o'er her fellows shows.

The measure done, I'll watch her place of stand,
And, touching hers, make blessed my rude hand.
Did my heart love till now? Forswear it, sight!
For I ne'er saw true beauty till this night.

  Task 5

In this task you will:

- examine Shakespeare's use of language.

1 In pairs, read through the speech and underline the words you do not know.

2 Work together using the resources available to you. Try to work out the meaning of the speech. Share your ideas with the rest of the class.

3 Romeo uses similes and metaphors to describe Juliet's beauty. Find examples from the speech.

4 This speech is rich in imagery. Choose three images from the speech and draw them.

5   Write notes explaining how these three images are used in the speech.

6   What does Romeo's language tell us about his character?

7   Construct your own metaphors/similes to describe someone you find attractive. Here are some examples.

- Fifty Cent's teeth sparkle like diamonds.
- Rebecca is as funny as a monkey roller skating.

After the ball Romeo leaves, but before he goes home he returns to see Juliet once more. She is standing on her balcony thinking about the evening's events and the man she's just met.

Juliet:	O Romeo, Romeo! wherefore art thou Romeo? Deny thy father and refuse thy name. Or, if thou wilt not, be but sworn my love, And I'll no longer be a Capulet.
Romeo:	I take thee at thy word. Call me but love, and I'll be new baptized. Henceforth I never will be Romeo.
	…
Juliet:	How camest thou hither…? The orchard walls are high and hard to climb, And the place death, considering who thou art, If any of my kinsmen find thee here.
Romeo:	With love's light wings did I o'erperch these walls. For stony limits cannot hold love out…

Task 6

In this task you will:

- make predictions
- work together in a group to write a script and perform it.

What happens next? Does she send him away? Are they discovered? Do they plan a future together?

1   In pairs, write the rest of this scene. You can use modern day language.

2   Once you have written the script, experiment with performing it in front of the rest of your class.

Here is an extract from Juliet's blog that reveals what happened that night on the balcony with Romeo.

> Tonight was the best night of my life. I met the most amazing man ever, Romeo Montague! 😊
>
> It all began at the ball. At first I didn't notice him. I was trying to avoid Paris, the guy my mum and dad want me to marry, when this gorgeous guy approached me. He took my hand and said it was like a holy place and his hand was unworthy to touch it. Not the most romantic chat up line, but at least it was original!
>
> Thankfully it was a masked ball so when my mum came looking for me to dance with Paris I just switched masks with my friends. Ingenious eh? 😉
>
> We talked and danced for what seemed like ages. Then came the best part. Romeo kissed me and it was by the book, perfect! Just then my silly old nurse came in. She said my mum was looking for me. I went off to find her but when I came back he was gone! I was heartbroken, but the worst was yet to come. My nurse told me his name is Romeo and he is a MONTAGUE. Talk about bad luck; trust me to fall for the only son of my dad's biggest enemy, my only love sprung from my only hate. ☹️

When I went to bed I couldn't sleep, every time I closed my eyes I saw his face. I had just gone out on my balcony for some air, when I heard a noise in the undergrowth. I looked down and was amazed. You'll never believe who had jumped the walls of the orchard just to see me: ROMEO!!

We talked, although not too loudly, about the fact he is a Montague and I am a Capulet. We decided that in the end it doesn't really matter. After all, a rose is still a rose and smells just as sweetly if it were named anything else. I said that. Pretty clever, eh!

He told me that he loved me and would rather die than be without me. We could've talked all night but finally he had to go, it was such sweet sorrow.

Just before he left I decided to see if he really loved me. I said that if he was serious we should get married and he agreed. We are both so excited. After he left he was going straight away to see his priest and make arrangements for the wedding.

I know, I know, it's all a bit sudden, but I've never felt like this before. Tomorrow he's going to send for me and we're going to be married. Can you believe it, me, a married woman and only thirteen! So, all I have to do now is find something to wear.

http://julietcapulet.blog.co.uk

Task 7

In this task you will:

- examine evidence
- make links between cause and effect.

1   Who does Juliet try to avoid? Explain why she may not want to see him. (Tip: How would you feel if your parents chose your partner?)

2   How does Juliet feel when she learns Romeo is a Montague? Why would this be a problem for the couple?

3   What does Juliet mean when she says 'a rose is just a rose'?

4   What have Romeo and Juliet decided to do?

5   What problems do you think Romeo and Juliet will encounter if they decide to go ahead with this plan? What are their alternatives?

6   Can you think of any other reasons why it might be difficult for someone to marry or be with their partner?

7   Write the comment you would leave on Juliet's blog.

Even though *Romeo and Juliet* was written over four hundred years ago many of the themes are still relevant to people today.

  Task 8

In this task you will:

- work in groups managing your own learning.

1 In pairs, discuss what you understand by the words 'love' and 'hate'.

2 How are these themes explored in *Romeo and Juliet*?

3 Make a collage or a multi-media presentation of song lyrics, magazine articles, poems, and films, etc. that focus on one or both of these themes.

4 What have you learned about why artists address these themes in their work?

The big fight

In this play the theme of love is never too far away from the theme of hate. On his way back from his marriage to Juliet, Romeo meets a cousin of Juliet's, Tybalt. Tybalt knows that Romeo and his friends gate-crashed the masked ball and is out for revenge. He has just been involved in a row with Romeo's best friend, Mercutio. In the course of this argument Mercutio has been stabbed.

Benvolio:	O Romeo, Romeo, brave Mercutio's dead! That gallant spirit hath aspired the clouds, Which too untimely here did scorn the Earth.
Romeo:	This day's black fate on more days doth depend. This but begins the woe others must end.
Re-enter TYBALT	
Romeo:	Alive, in triumph, and Mercutio slain! Away to heaven, respective lenity,

And fire-eyed fury be my conduct now!
Now, Tybalt, take the 'villain' back again,
That late thou gavest me. For Mercutio's soul
Is but a little way above our heads,
Staying for thine to keep him company.
Either thou or I, or both, must go with him.

Tybalt: Thou, wretched boy, that didst consort him here,
Shalt with him hence.

Romeo: This shall determine that.

They fight; TYBALT falls, he is dead

Benvolio: Romeo, away, be gone!
The citizens are up, and Tybalt slain.
Stand not amazed. The Prince will doom thee death
If thou art taken. Hence, be gone, away!

Romeo: O, I am fortune's fool!

  ## Task 9

In this task you will:

- manage information
- be creative.

1 Why are Romeo and Tybalt angry with each other?

2 Copy out the phrase that shows Romeo realises he has done something foolish.

3 Make a list of the consequences this act will have on the lives of the characters in the play, for example

   Romeo → will have to leave Verona or he will be sentenced to death

   Juliet →

4 Write some questions that you would like to ask Romeo. Choose one of your classmates to sit in the hot seat as Romeo.

Task 10

In this task you will:

- work in groups
- use ICT.

Work in groups to produce a news report on the big fight for the evening's news. Make notes on

- the headline for the story – it should be short but informative
- how the story will be reported; remember to include: who, what, when and why
- questions for eyewitnesses, character references for Romeo and Tybalt
- statements from the houses of Capulet and Montague
- the Prince's reaction to the day's events.

Juliet's dilemma

Juliet's father has arranged for her to marry Paris. Her mother arrives with news of her forthcoming wedding to Paris.

Lady Capulet:	I'll tell thee joyful tidings, girl.
Juliet:	… What are they, beseech your ladyship?
Lady Capulet:	Marry, my child, early next Thursday morn, The gallant, young and noble gentleman, The County Paris, at Saint Peter's Church, Shall happily make thee there a joyful bride.
Juliet:	… He shall not make me there a joyful bride. I wonder at this haste; that I must wed Ere he, that should be husband comes to woo. I pray you, tell my lord and father, madam, I will not marry yet;
Lady Capulet:	Here comes your father. Tell him so yourself, And see how he will take it at your hands.

Enter CAPULET and Nurse

Capulet: …How now, wife!
Have you deliver'd to her our **decree**?

Lady Capulet: Ay, sir; but she will none, she gives you thanks.
I would the fool were married to her grave!

Capulet: …How! Will she none? Doth she not give us thanks?
Is she not proud? Doth she not count her blest,
Unworthy as she is, that we have wrought
So worthy a gentleman to be her bridegroom?

Juliet: Good father, I **beseech** you on my knees,
Hear me with patience but to speak a word.

Capulet: Hang thee, young **baggage**! Disobedient wretch!
I tell thee what – get thee to church a' Thursday,
Or never after look me in the face.
Speak not, reply not, do not answer me!

My fingers itch. Wife, we scarce thought us blest
That God had lent us but this only child.
But now I see this one is one too much,
And that we have a curse in having her.
Out on her, **hilding**!

Look to't, think on't, I do not use to jest.
Thursday is near. Lay hand on heart. Advise.
An you be mine, I'll give you to my friend.
An you be not, hang, beg, starve, die in
the streets,
For, by my soul, I'll ne'er acknowledge thee,
Nor what is mine shall never do thee good.
Trust to't, bethink you. I'll not be forsworn.

Juliet: Is there no pity sitting in the clouds
That sees into the bottom of my grief?
O, sweet my mother, cast me not away!
Delay this marriage for a month, a week.
Or if you do not, make the bridal bed
In that dim monument where Tybalt lies.

Lady Capulet: Talk not to me, for I'll not speak a word.
Do as thou wilt, for I have done with thee.
…

Juliet: I'll to the Friar to know his remedy.
If all else fail, myself have power to die.

Glossary

decree: order or decision
beseech: I ask
young baggage: worthless
girl
hilding: hussy

Task 11

In this task you will:

- work in groups to examine the power of Shakespeare's language.

1   Mark the point in this scene where Juliet's father's attitude and his language change.

2   Make a list of the insulting comments made by Juliet's father.

3   In groups of three act out this scene. You can shorten it if you wish but think carefully about what needs to remain. Consider how best to show the relationship between the three characters.

4   When you have completed your work on this scene, think about the following: What does this scene tell you about the power fathers had over their daughters in Shakespeare's time? Do fathers still have the same power over their children today? Should parents have more power over their children or less?

Juliet is desperate. She goes to see Friar Lawrence, who married her, to get advice on what she should do. He tells her she should.

Glossary

vial: small glass bottle
distilled liquor: alcoholic spirit

> Go home, be merry, give consent
>
> To marry Paris. Wednesday is tomorrow.
>
> Tomorrow night look that thou lie alone.
>
> Take thou this **vial**, being then in bed,
>
> And this **distilled liquor** drink thou off;
>
> No warmth, no breath, shall testify thou livest.
>
> And in this borrowed likeness of shrunk death
>
> Thou shalt continue two-and-forty hours,
>
> And then awake as from a pleasant sleep.

Task 12

In this task you will:

- consider problems and how to solve them.

1 Summarise the Friar's plan in your own words.

2 Is this a good plan? Are there any problems with it that Juliet and the Friar have not thought about?

3 Can you come up with a better plan?

4 This plan will only work if the Friar lets Romeo know about it. Write the Friar's letter to Romeo explaining the plan for him and Juliet to be together again.

 # Task 13

In this task you will:

- perform in role.

Before Juliet drinks the potion she is worried and thinks about the outcome of her actions.

Make a list of all the things she might be thinking about at this point in the play. Present these ideas using the conscience alley technique.

A lightning before death

Romeo returns to Verona as he hears news that his beloved Juliet is dead. Unfortunately, he did not receive the Friar's letter so he is unaware of Juliet and the Friar's plan.

When he learns that Juliet is dead he decides his life is not worth living without her. He buys some poison, but before he drinks it he goes to see her one last time as she lies 'dead' in her tomb.

Romeo:	O my love, my wife! Death, that hath suck'd the honey of thy breath, Hath had no power yet upon thy beauty. Thou art not conquer'd. Beauty's ensign yet Is crimson in thy lips and in thy cheeks, And death's pale flag is not advanced there.
	…Eyes, look your last!
	Here's to my love!
	Drinks Thy drugs are quick. Thus with a kiss I die.
	Dies
Juliet:	What's here? A cup, closed in my true love's hand? Poison, I see, hath been his timeless end. O churl! drunk all, and left no friendly drop To help me after? I will kiss thy lips. Haply some poison yet doth hang on them To make me die with a restorative.
	Kisses him

Thy lips are warm.

O happy dagger!

Snatching ROMEO's dagger

This is thy sheath;

Stabs herself

there rust, and let me die.

Falls on ROMEO's body, and dies.

 Task 14

In this task you will:

- discuss your response to the end of the play in groups.

1   Will the feud continue after the deaths of Romeo and Juliet?
2   Do you like this ending? Can you think of an alternative?
3   What is Shakespeare trying to say about love and hate in this play?
4   Are any other themes explored in this play?

Word bank
Here are some interesting words from this unit.

feud (n)	theme (n)	The challenge is that you will be able to:
metaphor (n)	imagery (n)	
prediction (n)	vial (n)	• spell them
suicide (n)		• understand them
simile (n)		• use them.

Unit review

Here we will:

- review your own work

- recognise your strengths and weaknesses.

Discuss these questions in pairs, or write your responses in your Writing Portfolio.

- Why are Romeo and Juliet described as 'star-cross'd'?

- Can you identify the main themes in this play?

- What messages about these themes does the playwright want you to think about?

- Why do you think this play still appeals to modern-day audiences?

- What did you learn about how to develop the role of a character?

- How well did you work with others during group work?

Unit 6: See hear! Stage and sound

What we will be doing

In this unit we will:

- ask questions

- work in pairs and small groups

- listen attentively

- read, make and perform scripts.

What we will be learning

In this unit we will learn:

- to understand the language, forms and purposes of different media

- how the medium can affect the interpretation and performance of a text

- how to select the medium of communication which suits the purpose

- how to deconstruct, understand meanings and construct similar texts

- about the vocabulary of different media.

Thinking skills and personal capabilities

In this unit we will:

- respond creatively to different types of media, individually and in groups

- solve problems

- share ideas and work together to organise the performance of different texts.

Writers who have a story or message which they wish to share with an audience can choose from a range of media: television, radio, theatre, internet, newspapers, magazines, and so on. In this unit, we will examine the possibilities and opportunities presented to writers by radio and theatre.

Consider the word **medium** and decide why it might be used when talking about radio, stage or screen.

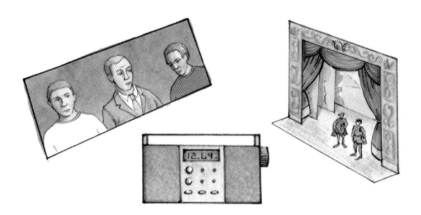

 Task 1

In this task you will:

*   sort words and phrases related to media.

Here is a list of words and phrases linked to the different media of radio, stage and screen. Sort them out under the headings of radio, stage and screen.

Note words which can be applied to more than one medium. (A dictionary might be useful for this task.)

> acoustics, announcer, balance, broadcast, set, bulletin, framing, proscenium arch, props, camera angles, station, trailer, in the can, props, lighting, outside broadcast, steady cam, close up, prompter, audio assistant, zoom lens, schedules, director, script, storyboard, studio, panning, running order, make-up, continuity editing, editor, transmission, voice-over.

Try to add to this with other words and phrases associated with radio, stage or screen.

Types of media

  Task 2

In this task you will:

- compare different types of media.

Use the table to consider the strengths and weaknesses of each medium.

Work in small groups.

	Strengths	Weaknesses
Radio Stage Screen		

  Task 3

In this task you will:

- discuss statements about drama and develop your own ideas.

A drama script on a page tells only half the story

Radio plays do not need real actors: readers will do

Shakespeare is boring

Directing a radio play is easier than doing one for television

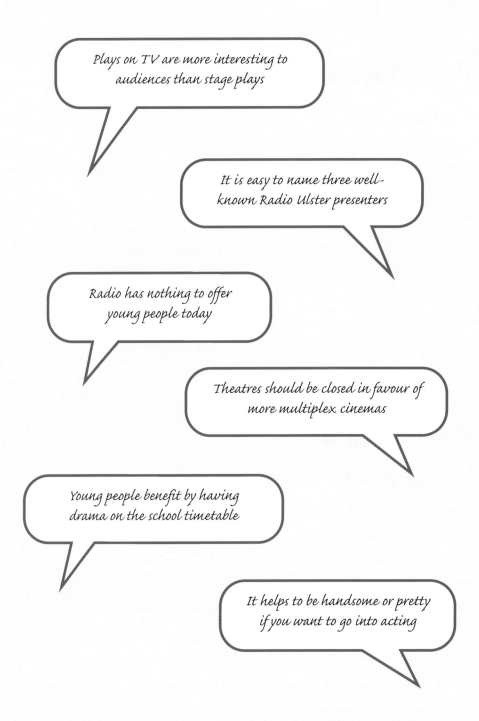

Plays on TV are more interesting to audiences than stage plays

It is easy to name three well-known Radio Ulster presenters

Radio has nothing to offer young people today

Theatres should be closed in favour of more multiplex cinemas

Young people benefit by having drama on the school timetable

It helps to be handsome or pretty if you want to go into acting

1   On your own, read each statement. Decide whether you agree, disagree or are uncertain.

2   Share your ideas with a partner.

3   Discuss what your conclusions tell you about drama.

4   List at least three things which you have learned about drama from your discussions.

Task 4

In this task you will:

- look at the strengths of the medium of radio.

Look at the diagram. Read and discuss the suggested strengths of radio as a medium of communication.

A radio play is free of all the limitations imposed by the stage or a film set. It can be set in any period, place or time.

Meanings are made solely through words and sounds/sound effects or music. Silence is equally important on radio. This strengthens the imaginative power of the radio.

Strengths of radio as a medium of communication

Stage and television provide all the images, colours and events for the viewer. The radio listener creates his or her own pictures. Radio is best appreciated by closing your eyes and using the words and sounds to make the story in your mind's eye.

Radio plays must be exciting, clear, engaging, otherwise the listener will stop listening.

The radio takes the listener inside the head of the character; it can expose what people are thinking.

It is cheaper than film or theatre! There are no sets or costumes and programmes can be broadcast in a small space with contributors seated on chairs.

Discuss two more strengths that could be added to the diagram.

Task 5

Survey of attitudes

In this task you will:

- use these questions to survey opinions and attitudes in the class.

1 What radio stations do you listen to regularly?

2 What are your favourite radio programmes?

3 When and where do you listen?

4 Why do you listen to radio programmes?

5 What television channels do you watch regularly?

6 What are your favourite television programmes?

7 When and where do you watch television?

8 Why do you watch television?

9 Have you been to see a stage play? Where? When? Do you have a favourite play?

10 Rate the three media according to how much you enjoy each one. (1 least to 5 most.)

Radio	Stage	Television
1 2 3 4 5	1 2 3 4 5	1 2 3 4 5

11 Explain and justify your ratings.

Present the attitudes and opinions of the class in the form of a poster or graph.

Task 6

In this task you will:

* read and respond to a text.

Read and discuss the text in pairs. Then answer the questions.

You're live on air

There are three things I know about radio. Okay, there are more than three, but bear with me.

The first is that if you are presenting a programme, you have to speak in a voice as close as you can get to your own. A clearer version of your own – and you can leave out the unfinished sentences, but you have to keep your own accent at the very least.

I knew that before I worked for Radio Foyle. It's common sense.

The second is that you speak as if you are talking to only one person. You don't say 'everyone' when addressing the microphone. You say 'you' because most people listen to the radio on their own.

I learned that from my first producer, Maureen Gallagher.

Third, the news, travel and weather items on a radio programme are called 'furniture features'. That means they are fixed in position. You do not move them about.

I learned that from a new book on radio skills called *Essential Radio Skills*.

The author, Peter Stewart, is a BBC trainer. I have been on the occasional BBC training course and they're nothing like this!

This book is laid out like a more sophisticated version of the 'For Dummies' series. The layout will appeal to those who can't digest large passages of writing. That covers most people who work in a radio station. Keep it short, keep it snappy.

We aspire to that on the radio. We don't always get there but this book does.

The emphasis throughout is on local radio, both commercial music stations and BBC local stations.

As someone who is still waiting for the tap on the shoulder, and hearing, 'Excuse me, you are not supposed to be working here,' it is interesting to read how programmes are supposed to be put together.

BBC training guides cover matters like legal advice, editorial policy, writing for radio – but I haven't yet seen one which tells you how to phone a potential guest for your programme.

So, you thought that radio presenters just gather a bunch of CDs, run into the studio and talk off the top of their heads in the spaces between the records. Well, they don't, apart from Gerry Anderson!

The process of putting together a programme is gone through in minuscule detail in this book. Some of it is depressingly businesslike.

A section on 'buying in' material to use in your links illustrates how uninspired some DJs can be. If you have the money to spend, you can get what is described as 'Show Prep Services': amusing things to say on your radio programme, such as comments on the day's news, horoscopes, fascinating facts. Stewart advises that you should change some of the material to make it more relevant to your audience. Otherwise it is like 'buying a Jamie Oliver cookbook and expecting to be a master chef'.

Reading this section, I found myself wondering what kind of numbskull has to be told things like 'change the location of the anecdote and use local places, streets and landmarks that your audience will recognise and connect with'. It is bad enough that some people use 'bought in' links, without having to be told to change London to Derry.

Some of the book does reassure you that the listener is unlikely to be fooled by such bluffers. 'Research shows that listeners can't abide presenters who are jokey with no wit, glib with no weight, trivial with no insight, or just plain dull.'

Having this book puts me in a difficult position. Having read it, I'm now full of ideas on how to do my job better. This will make me look good.

Or should I just buy half a dozen copies and pass them around Radio Foyle? The problem with that is it just might bring forward that tap on the shoulder!

Michael Bradley is a senior producer with BBC Radio Foyle and bass player with The Undertones.

Michael Bradley in Verbal,
27 February, 2007

1   What is the purpose of this text?

2   Who might be the audience which the writer has in mind?

3   From your responses to the first two questions, what do you think is the genre and form?

4   What do you learn about the skills needed to be a radio presenter?

5   What do you learn about Michael Bradley from what he has written and from the style and language of the text?

Soundscapes

  Task 7

In this task you will:

*   examine how sound can create meaning.

Sound is an important element of certain texts.

1   Close your eyes. What sounds can be heard in the classroom?

2   If you were to compose a 'sound postcard' of the most significant sounds which are typical of your school, what sounds would you collect? You might then share your 'sound postcard' with a neighbouring school.

3   What sounds would be needed to create a horror story?

4   When can sound be helpful when added to words?

5   When is sound more effective than words?

6   When is silence best?

Music and sound effects are often used in films or plays to create meaning or add to the meaning of the words or images.

7   Consider these two adjectives and try to work out what each means when describing sound: diegetic and non-diegetic.

8   When might a film, radio or stage use either type of sound?

9   Which kinds of sound will be diegetic and which are more likely to be non-diegetic?

10   In pairs or small groups, decide what these sounds might mean to the listener:

- footsteps
- breaking glass
- animated voices
- wind or rain
- orchestral music
- a bell sounding.

11   Consider other sounds which might make meaning.

Are sounds more important on radio than in a film or stage play? Explain your responses and share in small groups.

Under Milk Wood by Dylan Thomas

  Task 8

In this task you will:

- respond to words and phrases in the text of a speech
- prepare and present a dramatic reading.

This play is an unusual combination of voices and sounds that conjure up the dreams and waking hours of an imaginary Welsh seaside village within 24 hours. It introduces us to the people who live in Llareggub as they sleep, dream, wake up, go about their daily business and as night falls.

Here is part of the opening speech from the play, which was spoken by Richard Burton in the first radio performance for BBC Radio 3 in 1963.

Under Milk Wood

FIRST VOICE (very softly)

To begin at the beginning:

It is spring, moonless night in the small town, starless and bible-black, the cobblestreets silent and the hunched, courters'-and-rabbits' wood limping invisible down to the sloeblack, slow, black, crowblack, fishingboat-bobbing sea. The houses are blind as moles (though moles see fine tonight in the snouting, velvet dingles) or blind as Captain Cat there in the muffled middle by the pump and the town clock, the shops in mourning, the Welfare Hall in widows' weeds. And all the people

---

of the lulled and dumbfound town are sleeping now.

Hush, the babies are sleeping, the farmers, the fishers, the tradesmen and pensioners, cobbler, schoolteacher, postman and publican, the undertaker and the fancy woman, drunkard, dressmaker, preacher, policeman, the webfoot cocklewomen and the tidy wives. Young girls lie bedded soft or glide in their dreams, with rings and trousseaux, bridesmaided by glow-worms down the aisles of the organplaying wood. The boys are dreaming wicked or of the bucking ranches of the night and the jollyrodgered sea. And the anthracite statues of the horses sleep in the fields, and the cows in the byres, and the dogs in the wetnosed yards; and the cats nap in the slant corners or lope sly, streaking and needling, on the one cloud of the roofs.

You can hear the dew falling, and the hushed town breathing. Only *your* eyes are unclosed, to see the black and folded town fast, and slow, asleep. And you alone can hear the invisible starfall, the darkest-before-dawn minutely dew grazed stir of the black, dab-filled sea where the *Arethusa*, the *Curlew* and the *Skylark*, *Zanzibar*, *Rhiannon*, the *Rover*, the *Cormorant*, and the *Star of Wales* tilt and ride.

Listen. It is night moving in the streets, the processional salt slow musical wind in Coronation Street and Cockle Row, it is the grass growing on Llareggub Hill, dew fall, star fall, the sleep of birds in Milk Wood.

Dylan Thomas

1   Find the words and phrases from the speech which tell us:

* the time of day
* the season
* the weather
* the different places in Llareggub
* the people who live here
* what some of the people are doing.

2   What does Dylan Thomas think about the village? Find words or phrases which express his attitude to it.

3   In small groups, prepare and present a dramatic reading of this speech. Remember that it was written for radio.

Richard Burton   Dylan Thomas

Task 9

In this task you will:

- interpret a text using Reader's Theatre.

Before writing the play, Thomas wrote a short story which introduced many of the characters who were to appear later in his famous play. The short story is called, *Quite Early One Morning*.

1   Read the extract below.

2   Read the verses using the techniques of Reader's Theatre.

> Oh! the town was waking now and I heard distinctly, insistent over the slow-speaking sea, the voices of the town blown up to me. And some of the voices said:
>
> I am Miss May Hughes 'The Cosy', a lonely lady,
>
> waiting in her house by the nasty sea,
>
> waiting for her husband and pretty baby
>
>> to come home at last from wherever they may be.
>
> I am Captain Tiny Evans, my ship was the *Kidwelly*
>
>> and Mrs Tiny Evans has been dead for many a year.
>
> Poor Captain Tiny all alone, the neighbours whisper,
>
>> but I like it all alone, and I hated her.
>
> Clara Tawe Jenkins, 'Madame' they call me,
>
>> an old contralto with her dressing gown on.
>
> And I sit at the window and I sing to the sea,
>
>> for the sea doesn't notice that my voice has gone.
>
> Parchedig Thomas Evans making morning tea,
>
>> very weak tea, too, you mustn't waste a leaf.
>
> Every morning making tea in my house by the sea,
>
>> I am troubled by one thing only, and that's – Belief.

Open the curtains, light the fire, what are servants for?

I am Mrs Ogmore-Pritchard and I want another snooze.

Dust the china, feed the canary, sweep the drawing-room floor.

And before you let the sun in, mind he wipes his shoes.

I am only Mr Griffiths, very short-sighted, BA, Aber.

As soon as I finish my egg I must shuffle off to school.

Oh, patron saint of teachers, teach me to keep order,

and forget those words on the blackboard –'Griffiths Bat is a fool.'

Do you hear that whistling? – It's me, I am Phoebe,

the maid at the King's Head, and I am whistling like a bird.

Someone spilt a tin of pepper in the tea.

There's twenty for breakfast and I'm not going to say a word.

Thus some of the voices of a cliff-perched town at the far end of Wales moved out of sleep and darkness into the newborn, ancient and ageless morning, moved and were lost.

Dylan Thomas

Task 10

In this task you will:

* consider the effect a radio broadcast can have.

When dramatic news events happen, anywhere in the world, pictures and information are delivered, via satellite, straight into our homes. We can have rolling news 24 hours a day. If we wish, it is possible to gain access to several other channels or to the internet to find even more information. However, we have also learned to distrust the news, not to believe everything we hear and see on television. This is the modern world, but it was not always like this.

Before television became available to people, radio was in control of the airwaves. Broadcast in 1938, Orson Welles' radio production of *War of the Worlds* which was adapted from the science fiction novel of the same name, written by H G Wells in 1898, has gone down in history as the cause of the greatest mass panic of all time.

1 Work in small groups to find out what happened.
2 Can you explain why this radio play had such an effect on the audience?
3 Could such an event happen today?

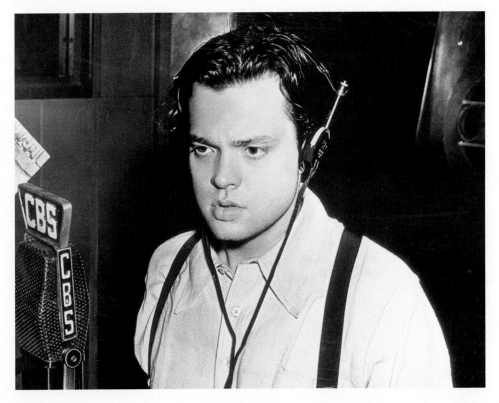

Orson Welles

Task 11

In this task you will:

- look at different ways of staging a dramatic text.

When a writer decides to present a text on stage, he or she must be aware of the conventions of this medium: how a theatre stage provides different challenges from those presented by radio where sound is of primary importance.

1   Discuss what you think *theatrical conventions* are and how they present different challenges for a writer.

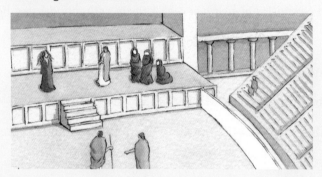

There are many ways to present or arrange a performing area or stage, and different ways of arranging the auditorium, where the audience sits. Here are four possible arrangements:

Open stage

The stage is at one end of the theatre and the audience face the same way.

Proscenium

An open stage with a picture frame or proscenium arch and perhaps an orchestra pit which separates audience from performers.

Theatre-in-the-round

The stage is in the centre and the audience sit around the stage.

Traverse staging

The audience sits on two sides of the stage, so they are looking at each other as well as at performers.

2   Draw a simple representation of each of these arrangements. It is important to select the most suitable arrangement when presenting a drama.

Task 12

In this task you will:

- work together in groups to stage a scene from a play.

Here are three play openings. In small groups, choose one.

Stage this opening and select the most appropriate method of staging arrangement.

The Tempest

Act 1 Scene 1: *On a ship at sea. A storm with thunder and lightning.*

Enter a Shipmaster and a Boatswain.

Master: Boatswain, –

Boatswain: Here, Master: what cheer?

Master: Good: Speak to the mariners: fall to't yarely, or we run ourselves aground; bestir, bestir. *(Exit).*

Enter Mariners.

Boatswain: Heigh, my hearts; cheerly, cheerly, my hearts; yare, yare: take in the topsail; 'tend to the master's whistle. – Blow till thou burst the wind, if room enough!

Blood Brothers by Willy Russell

Act One: *The overture comes to a close.*

Mrs Johnstone (singing): Tell me it's not true.

Say it's just a story.

The Narrator steps forward.

Narrator (speaking): So did y' hear the story of the Johnstone twins?
As like each other as two new pins,
Of one womb born, on the self-same day,
How one was kept and one given away?
An' did you never hear how the Johnstones died,

Never knowing that they shared one name,
Till the day they died, when a mother cried
My own dear sons lie slain.

Observe the Sons of Ulster Marching Towards the Somme by Frank McGuinness

Part 4: BONDING

A trench, the Somme. McIlwaine, the Younger Pyper and Millen are awake. The others sleep.

McIlwaine: You'd think they were dead, it's that quiet.

Pyper: Yes.

Millen: When do you think word'll come?

Pyper: When we're ready.

Millen: What have we to do with it?

Pyper: We do the attacking.

Millen: We don't do the ordering.

Pyper: You above all are not beginning to panic, Millen?

Millen: I've been panicking since the last leave, Pyper.

McIlwaine: There won't be much of daylight before we're going over.

Millen: I think this is it. I think this is going to be the end.

Pyper: Millen, for Christ's sake.

Millen: I can't help it. I know this time.

McIlwaine: Nobody knows nothing here.

Pyper: Any officers about?

McIlwaine: One passed twenty minutes ago. Told us to get some rest.

Millen: I saw him. Useless bugger. Surely to God they're not going to trust us with that piece of work. Where do they dig them out of anyway? Superior rank, is it? Superior, my arse.

1   Each group will present to the whole class, ensuring the staging is clear.

2   Discuss as a whole group each presentation, referring to:

- the suitability of the staging chosen
- the way the characters have been presented
- how the setting has been conveyed to the audience
- whether this is an old or modern play
- the events/what the play is about
- what you expect to happen next
- how you knew what was happening.

Stage or screen

  Task 13

In this task you will:

- look at the way music and other sounds can add effects to texts.

Love, jealousy, vengeance, murder – these are universal themes for poetry, story-telling and theatre, throughout history. Here is an opportunity to choose from different media techniques to explore dramatic emotions and events.

The text is an Irish song written in 1926, and said to have originated in Coleraine.

It tells the story of a love relationship which goes disastrously wrong because the parents and family of the young couple disapprove of the match. When a marriage is hastily arranged, tragedy follows.

> ### Johnny Doyle
>
> There's one thing that grieves me that I will confess,
> That I go to meeting and my true love goes to mass,
> But if it was so ordered, I would bear it with the toil,
> Through the world I would wander with you,
> Johnny Doyle.

I am a fair maiden all tangled in love,

My case I'll make known to the great God above;

I thought it a credit and I thought it no toil

Through the wide world to wander with you,

Johnny Doyle.

It happened to be on a Saturday night

When Johnny Doyle and I, we were going to take our flight,

My waiting maid being standing by, as plain as you may see,

She went unto my mother and she told upon me.

My mother she locked me in a room that was high,

Where no one could hear me nor no one could me spy,

She bundled up my clothes and she told me to begone,

So slyly and so slowly I put them on.

Five hundred bright guineas my father did provide

The day that I was to be Sammy Moore's bride.

And six double horsemen to ride to Ballintown

Unto one Mr Gordon's, where we lighted down.

We rode together till we came to the town,

Until Mr Gordon's we all dismounted down;

If theirs was the pleasure, mine was the toil,

For my heart I left behind me with young Johnny Doyle.

Soon as the minister he opened the door,

My earrings they bursted and fell till the floor,

And to fifty-five pieces my laces all flew,

I thought that my poor heart was going to break in two.

So behind my old brother I was then carried home,

And by my old mother conveyed unto my room,

And on my own bedside I leaned myself down,

And both sick, sore and weary my body I found.

'I'll send for Johnny Doyle, mother, if that he will come.'

'To send for Johnny Doyle, child, the way is far too long.'

'The journey is far and death will be my fate,

To send for Johnny Doyle, mother, it is far too late.'

'So mother, dear mother, make you fast the room door;

Till the breaking of the day, don't let in Sammy Moore.'

Early the next morning when young Sammy Moore arose,

And straight to his mistress' bedchamber he goes.

Folding down the clothes, he found she was dead,

And Johnny Doyle's handkerchief tied round her head,

Folding down the clothes, he found she was dead;

And a fountain of tears over her he did shed.

1 Read and discuss the ballad. Note how the songwriter has created:

- atmosphere/mood
- characters
- relationships
- build-up/anticipation.

2 How would music add to the effect of the words?

3 Decide on an appropriate tune which would support these lyrics.

4 Now work together in small groups. Select one of these tasks or share them around different groups in the class.

- Do a dramatic reading with sound effects, for radio, sharing the reading between four voices.
- Prepare a script for a stage play version, making decisions about set, costumes and sound effects.
- Use a storyboard to create a short fifteen-minute film of the text.

Word bank

Here are some interesting words from this unit.

acoustics (n)	producer (n)	The challenge is that you will be able to:
announcer (n)	production (n)	• spell them
broadcast (n)	proscenium (n)	• understand them
bulletin (n)	schedule (n)	• use them.
camera angle (n)	script (n)	
diegetic (adj)	sound effects (n)	
director (n)	techniques (n)	
editor (n)	theatre (n)	
performance (n)		

Unit review

Here we will:

- review your own work
- recognise your personal strengths and weaknesses.

Discuss these in pairs or small groups. Record your responses in your Writing Portfolio.

- What do you understand by the term 'media'?
- What are the strengths and weaknesses of sound, stage and screen as media for communication?
- How important is sound when constructing a story?
- What decisions does a drama director have to make before staging a play?
- What decisions does a playwright or script writer have to make before beginning to write?
- What else have you learned?
- What else would you like to know?

Unit 7: Hitting the right note

What we will be doing

In this unit we will:

- work individually, in pairs and small groups to consider a range of speeches
- actively engage in a variety of talking and listening activities to help develop your thinking about complex issues and ideas
- plan and make notes for a talk or speech, for example using intonation, gesture, humour.

What we will be learning

In this unit we will learn to:

- recognise a range of famous speeches
- know some techniques used by successful speech-makers
- understand how language can be used for a particular effect when delivering a speech
- understand the importance of considering purpose and audience when developing speeches
- understand how punctuation can be used to affect pace and tone in the delivery of a speech
- evaluate the success of a speech in terms of purpose, audience, organisation and clarity.

Thinking skills and personal capabilities

In this unit we will:

- do research and select the most appropriate information from a range of sources
- analyse, refine and structure information for an identified audience and purpose
- organise and plan how to go about a task, for example the delivery of a talk/speech.

Making speeches

  Task 1

In this task you will:

- work with peers to discuss and record information.

In groups of four or five, consider these questions and record your findings.

1   **When** do people make speeches?
2   **Why** do they make speeches?
3   Can you think of any **famous speeches** that you have heard? Consider at least one example.
- **Who** gave it?
- **What** was the occasion?
- **When** was it given?
- **Why** was the speech given, that is what was the purpose?
- **Who** was the audience?

Share information with the rest of the class.

Task 2

In this task you will:

- make connections and generate possible solutions.

1 With a partner, look at these lists and try to match each famous person to the famous phrase with which they are associated.

LIST A	LIST B
1 'I have a dream…'	A Mark Antony (in Shakespeare's *Julius Caesar*)
2 'Is this a dagger I see before me?'	B Gandhi addresses Indian National Congress
3 'Friends, Romans, countrymen, lend me your ears…'	C Mohammed Ali (former heavyweight boxing champion of the world)
4 'One small step for man, one giant leap for mankind'	D Roosevelt – Pearl Harbor Address
5 'Until we stand in the fields with the millions that toil each day under the hot sun, we will not represent India…nor will we ever be able to challenge the British as one nation'	E Martin Luther King (American Civil Rights campaigner in 1960s)
6 '…since the unprovoked and dastardly attack by Japan on Sunday, December 7th, 1941, a state of war now exists between the United States and the Japanese empire'	F Mother Teresa
	G Winston Churchill
7 'Brothers: What we do in Life echoes in Eternity…'	H Neil Armstrong (first man on Moon)
8 'I am the greatest'	I Bono
9 'Never, in the field of human conflict, has so much been owed by so many to so few…'	J Lenin
10 'A lie told often enough becomes the truth'	K Macbeth…in Shakespearean play.
11 'In that moment, I started this journey. In that moment, I became the worst thing of all: a rock star with a cause'	L Movie speech from *Gladiator*
12 'I know God will not give me anything I can't handle. I just wish that He didn't trust me so much.'	

2   Use your research skills to find a well-known phrase by a famous person. This quote can be from a politician or an actor in a film, play or television.

Get examples from the internet if you can! See if your partner can identify who said it and why.

www.famousquotes.me.uk/speeches/index.htm

3   Speeches are often developed with a particular purpose and audience in mind.

List some of the reasons why (purposes) speeches are given in the table and try to give an example of each. (You can use examples from Question 1 to give you some ideas.)

Purpose	Example
To entertain	*Wedding speech*

Features of an effective speech

  Task 3

In this task you will:

- examine evidence, and investigate cause and effect.

Have you ever heard of **rhetoric** or **rhetorical questions**? Use your thesaurus or dictionary to check the meaning.

There are many rhetorical **techniques** or **devices** used by people in public speaking. For example, rhetoric tends to be used by politicians in order to **persuade us** to their point of view.

One rhetorical device that is often used in writing speeches involves putting ideas, statements or points in an argument into **groups of three,** with an emphasis being put in the third part.

1   Search the list (in Task 2) for an example of this device. What is it? Check your answer with a friend.

2   Look at this extract.

Good evening. Today, our fellow citizens, our way of life, our very freedom came under attack in a series of deliberate and deadly terrorist attacks. The victims were in airplanes, or in their offices: secretaries, businessmen and women, military and federal workers; moms and dads, friends and neighbours.

The pictures of airplanes flying into buildings, fires burning, huge structures collapsing, have filled us with disbelief, terrible sadness and a quiet, unyielding anger.

George W Bush, 11 September 2001.

- How many examples of rhetorical language can you identify?
- Try to explain why you think it is rhetorical.
- See if you can identify an example of the trick of putting words or phrases into **groups of three** for effect.

 **Task 4**

In this task you will:

- select and classify information.

Listen to a famous speech from a chosen internet site (some examples are given) or listen to speeches from an audio tape provided by your teacher.

www.americanrhetoric.com/speechbank.htm

www.famousquotes.me.uk/speechesindex.htm

1 Individually, listen carefully to the speech and decide:

- who is speaking
- the context
- the purpose of the address
- the audience
- what **conventions/techniques** are used by the speaker to put across his/her point.

2 Do you think the speech is effective? Outline your reasons.

3 Discuss your ideas with a partner and make a list of the conventions or techniques used by the speaker in this table.

Features of an effective speech

Glossary

valedictory: used in saying goodbye

 Task 5

In this task you will:

- manage information
- access and select evidence of effective speech making.

Read through this extract from Tony Blair's **valedictory** speech at the Labour Conference.

In pairs, discuss some of the **techniques** used and record these in your table from Task 4.

Tony Blair's speech

I'd like to start by saying something very simple. Thank you.

Thank you to you, our party, our members, our supporters, the people who week in, week out do the work, take the flak but don't often get the credit. Thank you, the Labour party for giving me the extraordinary privilege of leading you these past 12 years.

I know I look a lot older. That's what being a leader of the Labour party does to you!

Actually, looking round some of you look a lot older…

I may have taken New Labour to the country but it was you that helped me take it to the party, so thank you.

Something I don't say often enough – thank you to my family.

It's usual after you thank the family, you thank your agent and yes I want to thank him and through him the wonderful people of Sedgefield…

But above all else, I want to thank the British people.

Not just for the honour of being prime minister but for the journey of progress we have travelled together. Leaders lead but in the end it's the people who deliver.

 **Task 6**

In this task you will:

- work in pairs
- give and respond to feedback.

Read through the openings to these speeches.

1. Consider why **the opening** to a speech is particularly important.
2. Note down anything you think that makes these openings successful. Share your opinions with the rest of the class; be prepared to defend your views.
3. What is the **purpose** of each speech?
4. Record any important techniques used in your table from Task 4.

A

Mr. Vice President, Mr. Speaker, Members of Senate, and of the House of Representatives;

Yesterday, December 7th, 1941, a date which will live in infamy…the United States of America was suddenly and deliberately attacked by naval and air forces of the Empire of Japan…

Yesterday, the Japanese government also launched an attack against Malaya.

Last night, Japanese forces attacked Hong Kong.

Last night, Japanese forces attacked Guam.

Last night, the Japanese attacked Wake Island.

And this morning, the Japanese attacked Midway Island.

Roosevelt: *Pearl Harbor Address to the nation, December 1941*

B

Ladies and Gentlemen, I have it on very good authority, that the quest for perfection our society demands can leave the individual gasping for breath at every turn.

This pressure inevitably extends into the way we look. And of course, many would like to believe that Eating Disorders are merely an expression of female vanity – not being able to get into a size 10 dress and the consequent frustrations!

From the beginning of time the human race has had a deep and powerful relationship with food – if you eat you live, if you don't you die.

Diana, Princess of Wales: *27 April 1993*

C

Ladies and Gentlemen, I'd planned to speak to you tonight to report on the state of the Union, but the events of earlier today have led me to change those plans.

Today is a day for mourning and remembering. Nancy and I are pained to the core by the tragedy. We know we share this pain with all of the people of our country. This is truly a national loss.

Ronald Reagan: *The space shuttle* Challenger *tragedy address, 28 January 1986*

D

My name is Bono and I'm a rock star. Brighton Rock Star.

Excuse me if I appear a little nervous. I'm not used to appearing before crowds of less than 80,000.

I heard the word PARTY – obviously got the wrong idea.

Bono: *Speech to the Labour Party Conference, 29 September 2004*

E Mrs. Mongella, Under-Secretary Kittani, distinguished delegates and guests:

This is truly a celebration – a celebration of the contributions women make in every aspect of life: in the home, in their communities, as mothers, wives, sisters, daughters, learners, workers, citizens and leaders…

There are some who question the reason for this conference. Let them listen to the voices of women in their homes, neighbourhoods, and workplaces…

It is conferences like this that compel governments and people everywhere to listen, look and face the world's most pressing problems.

Hillary Clinton: *Remarks to United Nations 4th world conference on women,*
5 September 1995

F During my research – and yes, believe it or not, this was researched – I looked into the three key elements of a wedding day: first, the aisle, the longest walk you'll ever take; second, the altar, the place where two become one; and third, the hymns, to celebrate the marriage. I hope for Paul's sake that this explains why my daughter was whispering 'aisle, altar, hymn; I'll, alter, him' throughout the service.

Anonymous, *internet*

5 Decide on a topic that interests you, or an issue that concerns you, and **write the opening paragraph** for a speech on that topic.

Remember to consider your **purpose** and **audience**.

6 **Assess your opening** against the features that you have outlined in your table.

Task 7

In this task you will:

- select, classify and evaluate information.

Read the following speech, which was written by a Year 11 student.

> Good day Ladies and gents, today I'm going to talk to you on a matter close to my heart: the never ending debate as to *whether or not sport stars are just spoilt brats.* Beckham and Rooney spring to mind but there are countless others…
>
> In the UK, there are over three million kids living in abject poverty. These youngsters don't have adequate clothing (not to mention designer labels), food or shelter. Just contrast this with the life of infinite luxury a top footballer leads.
>
> Take for example David Beckham – this so-called sporting superstar earns the same in one week as a typical teacher earns in 156 weeks! Further, Beckham provides, more often than not, second-rate entertainment on the pitch and is merely a puny fashion icon off it! Indeed he has just as many 'followers of fashion' as he does following his football mastery. Is he really a good male role model for our children wearing those skirts?
>
> It is not just football that is becoming uncontrollably influenced by money. In athletics, many athletes are turning to illegal drugs in order to obtain prize money in their event. The widespread use of these drugs is causing the credibility of sport in general to be questioned.
>
> I feel that this topic is unlikely to ever be settled amicably. The financial rewards will most likely continue to increase even more, drugs will be taken and ticket prices will go 'sky-high'.
>
> I firmly believe that most sport stars are just spoilt brats and possibly need to go out to a country like Africa to experience what life is really like for those who have to really work for their next meal, for one simple piece of clothing, even to go to see a match!

1   In pairs, consider the effectiveness of the speech, that is what do you think is the speaker's purpose and has he succeeded? (Remember it is a first draft.)

Use the ideas in the table to aid discussion.

	Commentary – suggestions for redraft
Purpose and sense of audience	
Structure – layout/paragraphing	
Content/facts/statistics	
Techniques or conventions used	
Appropriate use of language	
Use of punctuation	
Tone – formal/informal	

2 Discuss your ideas for redrafting with a partner. Refer back to the information collected on your grid and, together, outline in note form the main points that you feel must be considered to make improvements to this speech.

Task 8

In this task you will:

- use thinking and problem solving skills
- examine evidence
- make links between cause and effect.

Read or **listen** to Rowan Atkinson's *politician's speech*.

1   What makes this funny?

2   When did you first begin to suspect it was not serious?

3   When were you certain it was *a spoof*?

4   Use the thesaurus or dictionary to research the meaning of the words *spoof* and *parody*. Try to give a definition of each.

5   What aspects of the original language are copied?

6   In the end, does it make a serious point?

7   Give examples of other people whom you think might use *parody* to *satirise* the content or the form of the original speech.

Persuasive speeches

 Task 9

In this task you will:

- read closely to discover the techniques used in persuasion.

Read these speeches: the first from *Henry V* and the other from William Wallace, played by Mel Gibson, in the film *Braveheart*. They were written to persuade people in a particular way.

1 Compare the techniques used and say how effective each speech is.

2 Share your understanding of the speeches with your class group.

He which hath no stomach to this fight,

Let him depart; his passport shall be made,

And crowns for convoy put into his purse:

We would not die in that man's company

That fears his fellowship to die with us.

This day is called the feast of Crispian:

He that outlives this day and comes safe home,

Will stand a tip-toe when this day is named,

And rouse him at the name of Crispian.

He that shall live this day, and see old age,

Will yearly on the vigil feast his neighbours,

And say, 'To-morrow is Saint Crispian:'

Then he will strip his sleeve and show his scars,

And say, 'These wounds I had on Crispian's day.'

We few, we happy few, we band of brothers;

For he to-day that sheds his blood with me

Shall be my brother; be he ne'er so vile

This day shall gentle his condition;

And gentlemen in England now a-bed

Shall think themselves accursed they were not here,

And hold their manhoods cheap whiles any speaks

That fought with us upon Saint Crispian's day.

Henry V, *Act 4 Scene 3*

You have come to fight as free men, and free men you are. What will you do with that freedom? Will you fight? Aye, fight and you may die, run and you'll live. At least a while. And dying in your beds many years from now, would you be willing to trade all the days from this day to that for one chance, just one chance to come back here and tell our enemies that they may take our lives, but they'll never take our freedom?

Braveheart (*1995*)

Task 10

In this task you will:

- share opinions with your peers
- respect and take personal responsibility for working with others.

Imagine you have been invited to prepare a speech to be delivered at the Northern Ireland Assembly to mark the **Year of Youth**. Your speech is supposed to represent the hopes and needs of the present generation of young people and this is your big chance to have your say!

Work in pairs or small groups.

- Spend some time thinking about the main things you want to say and perhaps one or two overarching messages that you feel are important to get across, for example **This speech is intended to persuade people that…**
- Have a running order of your main points and, next to them, jot down examples you might want to include.
- Rehearse each point as you compose it, to hear how it sounds, and ensure that your message is clear.
- Consider what tone you will adopt for your speech.
- There is no need to write the whole speech down in prose – just make notes which contain key words and reminders. You might want to use a concept map, a spider diagram or linear format.

Deliver your completed speech to the class. Invite comments from your peers, and discuss what you have learned in the process.

Note

features of effective speech making you have noted so far in this unit.

Tip

It is often easier to use prompt notes rather than a full script, because this makes it easier to look directly at your audience and assess their reactions to what you are saying. Also you can fill in the linking words from your natural speech.

Connectives

therefore
consequently
subsequently
furthermore
further to this
however
in conclusion

Word bank

Here are some interesting words from this unit.

		The challenge is that you will be able to:
rhetorical question (n)	persuade (v)	
rhetoric (n)	satire (n)	• spell them
repetition (n)	parody (n)	• understand them
spoof (n)	conventions (n)	• use them.
formal (adj)	techniques (n)	
informal (adj)	repetition (n)	
conversational (adj)		

Unit review

Here we will:

- review your own work

- recognise your personal strengths and weaknesses.

In this unit how well did you:

- understand the importance of purpose and audience

- recognise rhetorical devices in speeches

- identify persuasive techniques

- plan for your speech

- deliver your speech

- work with your peers to problem-solve and research information?

Unit 8: In short...

What we will be doing:

In this unit we will:

- read and deconstruct short stories
- discuss features of short stories
- write short stories.

What we will be learning:

In this unit we will learn to:

- recognise the features of a short story
- understand the use of clauses to extend sentences
- use the power of adjectives, adverbs, strong verbs.

Thinking skills and personal capabilities

In this unit we will:

- solve problems and make decisions
- manage information
- think creatively and organise ideas to produce stories.

Task 1

In this task you will:

- evaluate information.

    Have you heard or read any stories today?

    Did your friend tell you one?

    Did the History teacher?

    Did any other teacher?

    Did your parents?

What do you think a story is? Is this a story?

A teacher was giving a lesson on the circulation of the blood. He thought he would make it interesting for the students. He said, 'If I stand on my head the blood rushes to it and my face turns red. But if I stand on my feet they don't turn red. Why do you think that is?'

One student waved his hand in the air and shouted, 'It's because your feet aren't empty!'

What makes it a story?

Keep a record of your answer in your portfolio.

Looking at short stories

  ## Task 2

In this task you will:

- experiment with ideas and language
- try out alternative approaches.

Here is a story in one sentence.

> He ate his dinner and died.

A good story captures your interest and makes you want to read on. To make this story more interesting the author could have added detail.

> The greedy footballer with hands like link boxes slurped and gobbled his way through ten plates of delicious pasta, which was drizzled with olive oil and covered with meatballs, before nature took its course and he burst wide open, forcing fellow diners to avert their gaze.

glossary

link box: trailer attachment for a tractor

The writer made this more interesting. Strong verbs were used, and powerful adjectives. More detail was given about the eater, his food, his surroundings, his fate.

Use colourful language, extra clauses, and powerful verbs to transform one of these sentence stories.

> The girl walked home from school and had an accident.

> The man caught a surprise when he went fishing.

> People moved around the city to avoid the flood.

> The farmer went to the market and lost his cow.

Task 3

In this task you will:

- communicate with a sense of audience and purpose
- sequence ideas.

Now that you have written a story in one sentence, try to write a story in exactly sixty words.

Your story may be in any genre you want.

Here are examples.

He walked slowly, limping. He seemed happy, and told jokes. I asked him about his limp. It happened, he said, when he fell off his bike in a race. He slowed near his garden gate and suddenly he stopped talking. He looked at the window. His face paled. I saw his father behind the glass, scowling. Suddenly I felt sick.

A man got three wishes.

'Ask for a son,' whispered his wife.

'No – riches,' demanded his father.

'Get my sight back,' pleaded his mother.

He was in a quandary, wanting to please everyone. After much thought, he smiled.

He went to tell the fairy his wish: 'Next year I want my mother to see my son in a golden cradle.'

Task 4

In this task you will:

- select the most appropriate method for the task
- give and respond to feedback
- seek advice.

Read aloud the second example.

Did your voice change in pace or tone or volume as you read it?

Where?

Why?

In groups, prepare to **read aloud** the story, *Royal Servant*. Each person takes a section of the story, reads it several times silently, noting how it should be read. Then read it aloud in your group.

Royal servant

The King of Kamera in Africa was a proud and stern man, feared by all his subjects. One day while sitting in his mud palace surrounded by fawning courtiers and watched by a multitude of people who had come to see him, he was suddenly overcome by a sense of grandeur and loudly declared that he was master of the world and that all men were his servants.

'You are mistaken,' said a frail voice. 'All men are servants of one another.'

A deathly silence followed the remark. The blood froze in the veins of the people assembled there.

Then the king exploded in anger.

'Who said that?' he demanded, rising from the royal stool. 'Who dares suggest that I am a servant?'

'I do,' said a voice in the crowd, and the people parted to reveal a white-haired old man, leaning heavily on a stout stick.

'Who are you?' asked the king.

'I am Boubakar,' said the man. 'We have no water in our village and I have come to ask for a well to be dug there.'

'So you are a beggar,' roared the king, striding down to where the man stood. 'Yet you have the temerity to call me a servant!'

'We all serve one another,' said Boubakar, 'and I will prove it to you before nightfall.'

'Do that,' said the monarch. 'Force me to wait on you. If you can do that I will have not one but three wells dug in your village. But if you fail, you'll lose your head.'

'In our village,' said the old man, 'when we accept a challenge, we touch the person's feet. Let me touch your feet. Hold my stick.'

The king took the stick and the old man bent down and touched the monarch's feet.

'Now you may give it back to me.' He said, straightening up.

The king gave him back his stick.

'Do you want any more proof?' asked Boubakar.

'Proof?' asked the king, bewildered.

'You held my stick when I asked you to and gave it back to me when I asked you for it,' said the old man. 'As I said, all good men are servants of one another.'

The king was so pleased with Boubakar's wit and daring that he not only had wells dug in his village but also retained him as an adviser.

African tale

Now retell the story, in your own words, to your classmates.

Planning your own short story

 Task 5

Prepare to **tell a story of your own** to your classmates.

To tell a story you need three things:

- a storyteller
- a story
- an audience.

You already have the first and third of these.

Now you need to decide what your story will be about and how you will tell it. To plan the story you are going to tell, use the grid below. This suggests where you might find ideas for a story and how you might begin or end it. Add as many ideas as you like in each section, and then choose those you think best.

Source of ideas	Content	Beginnings	Endings
school	trouble	Once upon a time…	They lived happily ever after.
films	happiness	Did you hear…?	And that's all I'm telling you.
visitors	monsters	Come here till I tell you…	If you want any more you can tell it yourself.
talk at mealtimes	winning	Long, long ago…	And that was that!
memories	magic	I remember it well.	So everyone was happy.

When you have made your choices, you need to organise your ideas.

Make notes to remind yourself what you intend to say. Use these notes as reminders – **but don't read from them**! Practise telling your story aloud.

In pairs, tell one another your stories. Give one another feedback.

This might include some of these points.

- Did the listener need more information?
- Did you need to slow down/speed up in places?
- Did you need to speak louder/softer in places?
- Did you need gestures?
- Did you maintain eye contact?

Now tell your story to the whole class.

 Task 6

In this task you will:

- sequence, order, clarify, make comparisons
- make new connections between ideas.

1 Do you think there are any differences between stories which are spoken and stories which are read?

2 Have they any common features?

Think of all the stories you have heard recently and what you have learned in this unit so far.

3 With your classmates, construct a wall chart of the features of a story. You can add to it as you learn more about the ways stories are created.

Task 7

In this task you will:

- make connections between ideas and information
- justify opinions and conclusions.

As you know from your storytelling, the way a story starts is important. It makes the reader want to read on.

The way a story ends is important; it must leave the reader satisfied and in some way tie in with the story start.

1　Match these story beginnings and endings.

2　What is the mood of the beginning?

3　What is the mood of the ending?

Beginnings

All that night Joe Maloney sweated, twisted and turned. He dreamed that engines roared and lights blazed. Men yelled, children screamed, dogs yelped. Metal hammered on metal. He dreamed that the surface of the earth was lifted and hung from great hooks in the sky. Beneath it, shapeless beasts danced in the dark. Then he lay dead still. Easy breath. Easy heart. He smelt sawdust, canvas, animal sweat, animal dung. Gentle noises, creakings and flappings. He felt something fingering his skull, someone whispering his name. He was about to wake up in some new place.

Buck did not read the newspapers, or he would have known that trouble was brewing not alone for himself, but for every tide-water dog, strong of muscle and with warm, long hair, from Puget Sound to San Diego. Because men, groping in the arctic darkness, had found a yellow metal, and because steamship and transportation companies were booming the find, thousands of men were rushing into the Northland. These men wanted dogs, and the dogs they wanted were heavy dogs, with strong muscles by which to toil and furry coats to protect them from the frost.

This adventure really began one early spring morning when I was fourteen years old. I remember it all so clearly from the moment when I stepped out into the still dark yard and went to unlock the stable door. The pony whinnied very quietly and stirred his feet in the straw of his bed. I remember looking up at the stars. Soon a soft light would come from the east, so gently that it would hardly be noticed at first. Then the birds would stir, and suddenly it would be day and the stars gone. I had always loved these early mornings when the pony and I travelled in warm companionship to the Saturday market in the town.

It was just an ordinary Saturday afternoon in October 1945. Except, in our house there was a flurry of activity and excitement. Mother was cleaning and polishing, trying to keep busy. An appetising smell of stew and dumplings wafted all around the small but neat kitchen. Father was coming home. He had been away for five long hard years, held captive in a prisoner of war camp in Germany. When peace was declared, he again was unfortunate to be moved along with many other poor souls to another prison camp, where he became very ill and had to spend many more months recovering. But today he was coming home.

Endings

But he is not always alone. When the long winter nights come on and the wolves follow their meat into the lower valleys, he may be seen running at the head of the pack, through the pale moonlight or glimmering borealis, leaping gigantic above his fellows, his great throat a-bellow as he sings a song of the younger world, which is the song of the pack.

That Saturday afternoon in October everything was alright in our house. The past five years seemed to vanish away, no more waiting, no more parting, we were a family once more. Daddy was home. I looked around the room at the shining, tear-stained faces of my mother, my sister and my brothers, and wondered if this was how life was – to be really, really happy you had to be awfully sad first. After sixty-plus years' experience, I think the answer may be yes.

At last we turned into our lane. The horse's hooves moved silently on the sand, and then we heard my mother's voice, high and melodious, calling her hens to come home. We turned into the farmyard, and there she was at the door. We climbed down out of the trap, and then we all went into the house together.

He leaned on his mum. He gazed into Corinna's dark eyes. With everyone in the garden, he began to sleep. The world beneath them turned towards the day. The tiger crossed the wasteland. It padded back to the forest through the night.

Task 8

In this task you will:

- examine evidence
- classify; justify opinions and conclusions.

Thinking of all the stories you have read and heard recently, and thinking of what you learned so far about short stories, read the following story, and annotate it to show the features of a short story. The wall chart from Task 6 may be helpful here.

The Sea

I have always loved the sea. Living in Africa, two hundred miles from the coast, the hunger to see great waters gnawed at me, relieved only by visits to the coast of Zululand, and that only for a short time. In the dry hills of Swaziland, I eked out the memory of the white surf of the Indian Ocean much as, as a child in Donegal, I would have nibbled a bar of chocolate, trying to make the pleasure last. But, as sure as the pleasure of the chocolate bar would end, so too the memories of the sea would lose their edge, and the hunger come back.

It was in Donegal that I first came to know the sea. We spent our holidays with my aunt. I spent my time at the quay, particularly every evening when the boats returned from fishing. One boat in particular I loved, the *Girl Mary*, and I pestered the crew – Jimmy the captain, Willie and Donald and

---

Liam – to let me go out with them. Willie came over one evening to check with my father and I was allowed to go.

The result was humiliation. I became so seasick that they had to bring the boat back and leave me off. They went back to their fishing and I went to my bed, where I cried in shame. For the rest of the week I avoided the quay. One thing I could not avoid was Mass on Sunday. Following my family, I was aware of men resting against the grass bank, talking till the last ring of the bell would take them into chapel, and I kept my head bowed. I heard my name called, and looked up. Jimmy was signing for me to come over. He handed my half a crown and said, 'You weren't there to get your share yesterday.'

The rest of the holiday passed in a haze. I met the boat every evening. After we landed the catch, I would walk with them to the pub, where they drank Guinness and bought me cola.

In late September I came back, late on a Friday night. First thing next morning I was on the quay, waiting with the others for Jimmy. He was late. The morning was wet and we decided to go out and wait on the boat. The moorings needed adjusting. As the others worked at them, Willie took out a hand line and said that if Jimmy didn't come soon, they would have to start dragging for him. They all laughed as Willie dropped the line with its heavy weight over the stern of the boat. He gave a pull and suddenly froze, his face paling. I looked over the stern in time to see a raft of bubbles forming on the surface. Liam, the youngest, reacted first, caught me under the arms and lifted me up to the quay. 'Go home now,' he said, and I ran, because, coming to the surface with the bubbles, I had seen the back of a fisherman's sweater.

I love the sea; but I fear it more.

Kevin Johnston

Does this story satisfy the 'w' words – Who? Where? What? When? Why?

Add anything you have learned from this story to the wall chart.

Looking at plot and theme

  Task 9

In this task you will:

- make new connections between ideas and information
- examine evidence
- justify conclusions.

Sometimes the writer of a story wants to do more than just give the facts of the story. He/she may want to get a message across. This is known as the **theme** of the story.

For example, the theme of the story of *Cinderella* may be one of trust, or that in *Little Red Riding Hood* might be disobedience.

Think back to *The Sea*. What was the **plot**? What was the theme?

Read this story. What is the plot? What is the theme?

> **glossary**
>
> **plot:** the organisation of incidents and events in a story
> **theme:** the central idea of a piece of writing

Making haste slowly

A trader bought a large number of coconuts at a village and, loading them onto his horse cart, set off for home. Encountering a boy a little later, he asked him how long it would take to reach the main road.

'Go slowly and you'll reach it in ten minutes,' replied the lad, 'but if you go fast it'll take you half an hour.'

'Fool!' shouted the trader and drove away at breakneck speed.

Fifty metres down the road one of the wheels struck a stone. The jolt sent the coconuts flying in all directions. It took the man a long time to gather all the coconuts and put them all back in the cart. Afterwards, he climbed back wearily into the driver's seat and, with the little boy's words ringing in his ears, drove slowly and cautiously the rest of the way.

Tale from the Philippines

In pairs, discuss stories you have read or heard and try to work out the themes.

Task 10

In this task you will:

- focus, sustain attention and persist
- break the task into subtasks
- use a range of methods to collate, record and represent information
- use ICT.

Sometimes the theme is explicit; at other times the reader/listener has to work it out. A theme can help you understand something better or to realise that others have felt as you do.

Story is universal. Themes recur in various cultures, and issues which appeal to a variety of readers are dealt with.

Research stories from various parts of the world. Try to find three with a similar theme.

Copy and complete the table.

	Country of origin	Title	Genre	Plot/Theme
Text One				
Text Two				
Text Three				

Task 11

In this task you will:

- organise and plan how to go about a task
- sequence, order, classify; experiment with ideas and language
- communicate with a sense of audience and purpose
- use ICT.

Write a short story, bearing in mind what you have learned about the features of a short story. Remember, for example, the five 'w' words, the genre you would like to explore, and the preferred point of view.

As an aid to your writing, consult the class wall chart and the notes you have kept in your Writing Portfolio.

 Task 12

In this task you will:

- review personal targets
- respect the views and opinions of others
- be fair.

- In pairs, consider one another's stories in the light of what you have learned in this unit and using criteria agreed by the class. You may use your wall chart to help formulate the criteria.
- Define a short story. Retain this definition in your Writing Portfolio.

Word bank

Here are interesting words from this unit.

character (n)	introduction (n)	The challenge is that you will be able to:
protagonist (n)	conflict (n)	• spell them
theme (n)	resolution (n)	• understand them
setting (n)		• use them.
organisation (n)		

Unit review

Consider these questions:

• How well did you tell a story?

• Do you understand the features of a short story?

• Did the story you wrote meet the agreed criteria?

• How well did you give and respond to feedback?